EBBSFLEET
UNITED
FOOTBALL CLUB 08

THE F.A
TROPHY
FINAL
2008

MARCHING TO
WEMBLEY

THE F.A
TROPHY
FINAL
2008

MARCHING TO
WEMBLEY

the fleet
@wembley

EBBSFLEET UNITED – FA TROPHY WINNERS 2008

JaM
BOOK PUBLISHING

the**fleet**@wembley
First edition published in 2008 by **JaM BOOK PUBLISHING**
in association with Ebbsfleet United Football Club

Text & Design © **JaM BOOK PUBLISHING** 2008
Art Direction & Design: Jim Lockwood
Official Club Photography: Dave Plumb
Pitchside Photography: Matthew Ashton & Catherine Ivill/AMA

For all queries concerning this publication please write to:
JaM BOOK PUBLISHING
PO Box 979
Shrewsbury
SY3 7XB
UK
info@jambookpublishing.com
www.jambookpublishing.com

Printed in Singapore 2008

15 14 31 10 05 08 12

A CIP catalogue for this book is
available from the British Library

ISBN 978-0-9556518-1-6

the fleet
@wembley

EBBSFLEET UNITED – FA TROPHY WINNERS 2008

edited by **SIMON DENTON**

CONTENTS

EDITOR'S NOTE

Twelve months ago, if someone had foretold that in a year's time I would be editing a book on Ebbsfleet United, I would have found it hard to believe. Even after my first visit of the 2007/08 season to Stonebridge Road on a swelteringly hot late August afternoon you would have got very long odds on this happening. On that occasion, I was on the open visitors terrace watching the Fleet defeat my own Halifax Town 1-0 in a game that wasn't a particularly good advert for Conference football. I left the ground feeling quite ill. It was probably the heat as much as anything but I was also agonising over how the loyal Halifax Town fan base would react to the possibility of been taken over by an internet website called MyFootballClub.co.uk (MyFC). At this point, only a select few knew of the plans afoot. It had to be this way as there was also a protracted potential takeover by a locally based Consortium happening at the same time. Yorkshire folk are well known for being quite blunt and stuck in their ways although even I wasn't prepared for the initial backlash against MyFC that lit up the internet messageboards like never before. In the end, all the prevarication from a select few was of no consequence as the person who owned the major shareholding decided to go with the Consortium.

When it became clear that Halifax Town was not going to be the club to benefit from MyFC, I felt that I was too far down the road with MyFC just to cast it to one side. Almost immediately, I became involved with the articles section of the MyFC website and have been looking after it ever since, hence the reason why I have been afforded the privilege of editing this publication.

So why am I telling you this in a book about Ebbsfleet's big day out at Wembley for the FA Trophy Final? Two reasons really, the first is to set the scene as to why a die hard Halifax Town fan has chosen to dedicate so much of his time to Ebbsfleet United and MyFC and, secondly, to try and demonstrate how an 'outsider' can empathise and understand what the longstanding Ebbsfleet supporters must have gone through, both in the early days of the MyFC takeover, and probably also at Wembley when 25,000 Ebbsfleet fans turned up from all over the world. To 'go global' overnight is a difficult concept to take in for anyone but to also have unknown faces looking to have a say in your club and then take part in your big day as if they had been there for years must have felt quite strange, to say the least.

Over the months that I have been editing the MyFC articles, I have detected an ever-increasing acceptance of the MyFC concept into the daily life of Ebbsfleet United. Whilst there are still likely to be challenges ahead, particularly around 'Pick the Team', I think we are all beginning to see and further believe that we have a viable alternative to the traditional 'one owner in charge' way of thinking. At Halifax Town, we have adopted the saying 'Fortune Favours the Brave'. In accepting MyFC, the former Ebbsfleet directors have shown that they were prepared to be brave and move outside of the traditional way of thinking as a way of moving their club forward. You only have to look at the contrasting fortunes of Ebbsfleet United and Halifax Town to see that fortune does indeed favour the brave!

So, moving on to the publication that you now hold in your hands. To complement the many pictures of the big day itself, I have put together a collection of articles that will hopefully help to illustrate how supporters new and old came together to celebrate Ebbsfleet's success. There are articles from long-standing Ebbsfleet supporters, full converts, occasional attendees and members making their first public appearance. All have their own take on how the day unfolded and the reasons why they were there.

Apart from, perhaps, a play-off final appearance, I don't think that Ebbsfleet and MyFC could have wished for a better end to the season than victory in a Wembley showpiece final.

It's been a fantastic first six or so months for Ebbsfleet and MyFC. In the words of a well known bank, most, if not all, of us are in this 'for the journey'. We now have a few weeks off to contemplate and evaluate what has happened before we start on the next leg in early August.

In closing, my thanks go to everyone who has made this publication possible. ✆

SIMON DENTON (ShaymanDownSouth)

The FA
TROPHY

EBBSFLEET UNITED
FOOTBALL CLUB
THE FLEET

THE OLD MAN
WITH THE BIKE

I never knew his name, the old boy with the bike. It was probably over 30 years ago when I first became aware of him. You could take bikes, dogs, footballs, anything into the ground in those days. Late one Saturday afternoon, I emerged from the centre stand tunnel, after a particularly gritty win, to see an old man with an ancient green bike, complete with old fashioned handlebars and a massive metal casing around the chain, standing beneath the open window of the home dressing room. He craned his neck up and yelled at the opening above him, his voice trembling a little in the higher pitch of age, "Well done, you red boys! Well played!"

He wasn't there after every game but you could bet your house he'd be under the window after any match where the boys in red had fought with every ounce of their being – grit and determination have always been valued virtues amongst the Stonebridge Road faithful. He'd have to be long dead by now and it must be at least a decade since I've seen him and his bike behind the stand.

Boxing Day 1971 was my first match. I'd heard the van drivers at my Saturday job talking about the Fleet and nagged my dad into coming along with me. Despite a gutsy performance, the boys in red were ultimately beaten 1-0 by a more accomplished Dartford but dad and I were hooked. At the start of the 1974/75 season, with four years at Exeter University ahead of me, I persuaded my mum to go too, afraid my dad would drift away without his regular companion. It wasn't all down to filial devotion; I wanted eye witness reports of the games I'd miss.

Anyway, come the end of that season, Brian Woolfe's mazy, lopsided runs through and round bewildered defences, Kenny Burrett's crunching tackles and enormous long range efforts on goal and Tony Weston lifting the Southern League Division 1 (South) Trophy had confirmed my mum as a Fleet fan too. All of which meant that my younger sister got dragged along as well and had much ribbing to endure at school the week a photo of her and Tommy Watson, her favourite player, appeared in The Gravesend Reporter.

What happened between then and now has been repeated in many homes and many hearts; the Fleet simply became a fundamental part of our life. I can remember travelling by bus and train throughout the south west during my university years to watch triumphs at Bideford and Minehead, as well as having to walk three miles in a torrential downpour from the old Huish to Yeovil Junction, after a 3-1 thumping (students didn't do taxis in those days.) My mind was with the Fleet's fortunes a few years later as I swam in Lake Galilee after finishing my kibbutz shift and when I rather rudely helped myself to a middle aged English couple's Sunday Telegraph on a beach near Tel Aviv only to learn that a 3-1 defeat at Barrow, where my mum had been amongst the Fleet faithful, had seen us relegated from the original top tier of non league football. As I've said, admission was not limited to humankind ⟫

○ Billy Westhead over the moon at Wembley
DAVID WESTHEAD

○ Half an hour before the game, the red side of the crowd outnumbers the yellow
NICK FISK

○ A big hand for The Fleet!
SIMON CLARIDGE

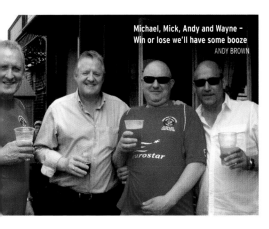

Michael, Mick, Andy and Wayne –
Win or lose we'll have some booze
ANDY BROWN

only in those days and so it was in the 80's that my parents' small though rather fierce dog became a regular fixture in the Centre Stand, later to be joined by our daughter's black and tan equivalent, during the time that my wife was the club's Commercial Director.

The funny thing is that, over all those years, the most ordinary away wins shine in my memory like they were yesterday. I can still see Brian Woolfe, Colin Norman and Peter Hearn scoring at a rain soaked Bideford in 1974 where I was one of just four Fleet supporters, whilst many of the home games – apart from the most glorious moments – are misty in the depths of time. Moments like these lit up my weekends and over time I learnt not to be embarrassed or prevaricate when people asked what team I supported. I came to understand that I was part of that select band that can call themselves real supporters whilst those who mocked from their lofty heights of professed allegiance to Arsenal, Liverpool or Man U were no more than followers and could never hope to be anything more.

I can't believe they really know what it's like ▶▶

Pre-Wembley nerves are quashed at The Globe, Baker Street
ALAN ELFORD

Andy Brown's friends and family being 'papped'
MAX NEWTON

THE TORCH

The players and staff at Burnham Beeches hotel before the trip to Wembley

⋂ The gang from Nottingham
⤺ Holding the flag for the Fleet, from left to right: Jim, Alan and Glenn
⤻ EUFC fans and members before the game: Lee Delaney at back; middle (from left) Steve Rose, Michael Rose, Jeff Chick (Barda), Ed Miller (Timechaser), David Pratt (Davpra) and Sebastian Juniper; Angela Massie at front (mysecondclub)
⤼ Firehazzard before the game on Wembley Way

Keza, Emma, Matt and Alfie
PAUL APPS

◑ Megan Holding and Robert Boyce before kick-off · ROBERT BOYCE
◔ Margaret Doran models the Fleet's commemorative T-shirt · TERRY DORAN
◔ The Glynne-Jones massive at the White Horse bridge · TIM GLYNNE-JONES

for their team – to be a part of them, something they have grown up with, or, as in the case of many Fleet fans, grown old with. Could they have felt as I did at the end of both matches against Aldershot or as I emerged from the tube station on that Saturday in May and began the walk up Wembley Way? I believe not, and why? Because their side will never, can never, be truly theirs in the way the Fleet is part of me and part of all those others who have followed them unconditionally through bad years and good.

And this is something which so many MyFC people have recognized; suddenly they too, though for different reasons to us old timers, are committed to something which, despite all the other things in their lives, will always be there and with which they can feel truly, personally involved. This is why for us the sight of Paul McCarthy lifting that Trophy aloft went far beyond how any Manchester United supporter, player and even Alex Ferguson felt when the Champions League was won in Moscow.

I cannot describe my feelings as I got up early on that morning and pulled on my first ever Fleet replica shirt though I know they were shared by many others who also had more than just themselves to take to Wembley that day. One supporter has told how he wore three Fleet scarves, two of which belonged to members of his family who had passed away. As for me, I called in on my mum's now empty bungalow for a few moments before my walk to the station and took with me the flag she waved at Villa Park. She died almost exactly a year ago, a Fleet fan to the last, like my dad who passed away nine years before her, also in May, and went to games even after Glaucoma had made him completely blind.

Whilst daughter and sister, my wife and her dad (who, as a boy, slid under the fence to watch Northfleet United play) made their way straight to the stadium, I calmed my nerves in The Metropolitan with my brother in law (and friends), a friend from my university days at Exeter so long ago (and more friends), a former work colleague (and daughter – both Welling fans most of the time) and Dick Durkin, better know to Fleet fans as the iconic Blind Bigot, a passionate Fleet supporter ever since their performance against his own Huddersfield Town half a dozen years ago. The rather fine *Exmoor Gold* helped me keep the emotions in check until we emerged from Wembley Park and I saw the sea of red and white stretching ahead of me right up to the famous arch; then I had to walk ahead so the rest could not see that my eyes were occasionally no longer dry.

If all the companions marching alongside me on that long walk had been visible to anyone else we would have looked a strange and motley crew: old and young, sighted and blind, human and canine. Perhaps, though, I wasn't the only one to hear the solid clank, clank of an ancient green bicycle being wheeled along. ◉

GRAHAM SIDWELL (Graham S)

CHAPTER 2
THE DAVS'
DAY OUT

The view down
Wembley Way from
the Corinthian lounge
TOM BROOKS

They say that timing is everything – not the case in our family where timing is largely irrelevant. If it's fashionable to be late then we are right up there with Gucci, Armani and their mates. Highly unlikely then that dad would turn up much before 8.30am to drive Jon and I down to London for the big day out. At least that's what we probably thought at around 2.30am after 'just one more go' on *Guitar Hero*, several bottles of wine and a healthy dose of groupies to look after (not mentioning any names – Di, Kylie, Angelina... x). Imagine our surprise when dad rang to say he'd be twenty minutes early. Admittedly, we were kind of hoping to get a little more sleep and that he'd eat a little into the extra hour leeway we'd put into our plans but, fair play to him, for the first time in living memory we could dream of arriving somewhere early. I'm no doubt in big trouble for writing that but could there possibly have been a better omen for the day ahead?

Twenty minutes later, bags were packed, music was chosen and, after settling down between the scarves and pennants draped around the inside of the car, we were on our way through the outskirts of Sheffield. So far so good. All we had to do now was to navigate down the M1 to Stanmore, park the car, get the tube, find the MyFC pre-match do and family gathering to meet our other two brothers, Chris and Beeb, who had wisely decided to stop in London the previous night with Vikki and Emma. What could possibly go wrong? We

were hoping for lots of hilarious 'fell asleep on the tube' stories to write about but, unfortunately, the whole day worked out as planned. Oh well, can't have everything.

The romantics among us wanted to see hordes of Fleet fans in a convoy down the M1 sporting their red shirts and showing their backsides to Torquay fans through the back window, somewhat of a tradition on a cup final day apparently. Geography dictated that this didn't actually happen given >>

⤴ **That first pint smile...**
ANTHONY DAVENPORT

ENTRANCES

HJKL MNP →

CLUB WEMBLEY 2

↻ What do you call a group of Davs?
ANTHONY DAVENPORT
↻ One of the many items of merchandise for sale on Wembley Way...   JEFF CHICK

that Torquay is a couple of million miles, give or take, south of the M1 but the expectation of seeing cars full of Fleet fans keeping their eyes peeled for yellow shirts in other cars kept us busy for many a mile. We eventually arrived at Stanmore station in good time and saw plenty of supporters from both sides parking up and making their way to the tube station. The atmosphere was friendly, conversations started up with the inevitable 'Are you going to the meet?' and it was at this point we got chatting to Meg and her dad who had travelled down from Norwich. Particularly noticeable were the red toothbrushes they were both proudly carrying, the significance of which was lost on dad and Jon. Meg definitely understood that carrying a red toothbrush around London may look a bit strange and explained it away by saying she did have an electric one at home!

The tube ride was uneventful, each passing station increased the butterflies in our stomachs and once we got to Wembley Park the significance of the day started to kick in, even more so with the first sight of the Wembley arch and being asked to stand with a young Torquay fan while his dad photographed him with some 'Ebbsfleet lads' as he put it, the first time anyone had referred to us as fans rather than owners. This was reinforced when we arrived at the MyFC do, hundreds of people of different nationalities and backgrounds simply enjoying a good day out, the fact that beer and bright sunshine were involved making it even more enjoyable!

It was a little bizarre at first to hear so many different languages and accents in one place but »

the topic of conversation never veered far from the universal language of football, whichever accent (or dialect) it happened to be in. The sun was beating down and, milk-bottle white being the colour of choice in Sheffield, sun cream was liberally applied. We spent time with a couple of knowledgeable guys from Zagreb in Croatia, one a member of MyFC, the other, referred to as his bodyguard, was just along for the ride. There was a certain distant familiarisation with usernamed shirts and avatar lookalikes and a lot of friendships looked like they were being cemented. The family gathering was complete when the rest of the clan turned up without incident, looking like they'd had several more hours sleep than we did. Still, if you want to be a rock god you have to put in the hours!

As the pints emptied and the minutes passed, pockets of people started to leave and make their way to the stadium; a swift drink later and we joined them. It was obvious from walking towards the stadium that there were more Ebbsfleet fans than Torquay and this was emphasised once into the ground with loads of Fleet supporters in the upper tier. At least they could take heart that their altitude nosebleeds wouldn't show on their shirts! Our seats were in a great position, second row back just to the side of the goal. Unfortunately, there wasn't much action at our end of the pitch and the crowd seemed quite subdued in the first half. The goal just before half-time changed that, the whole place went absolutely mental. A few

Mexican waves (aptly in keeping with our global reach) in the second-half brought the panto season forwards, especially when the Torquay fans refused to join in and were loudly booed. Towards the end of the game, as the party started to get going inside the stadium, the ball boy directly in front of us got his 15 seconds of fame. The fun-police in their orange vests wouldn't return the beach ball that had been punched, headed and toothbrushed over the barrier. Mr Ballboy took some cajoling but left his chair to throw the ball back into the crowd. Cue chants of 'ball boy is a legend, ball boy is a legend, na-na na na, na-na na na'. The look on his face afterwards was priceless.

The end of the game tortuously arrived and at the final whistle pandemonium ensued. It was around the time the trophy was being paraded that we heard a rumour that we'd been spotted on Sky's footage of the game by grandad. We made our way back up the M1, fuelled by a dirty burger, a warm beer, a well-deserved victory, and having made it unscathed through a thoroughly enjoyable family day out. We gathered around the Sky+ box back at the flat and we found proof that the rumour was indeed true. Just after the trophy presentation is a shot of the crowd with dad and his rhythmically-challenged eldest son next to him awkwardly moving his body with no regard for the music that is playing. Oh the shame. My mate Lee summed it up using a quote from Friends – 'Gloria Estefan was right – the rhythm IS going to get you...' ⊕

ANTHONY DAVENPORT (antdav)

⋒ **Wembley Way at 1.00pm** JACK HOWES
⮩ **Spencer diverted his stag do from York to Wembley to be at the match** SPENCER DOLMAN

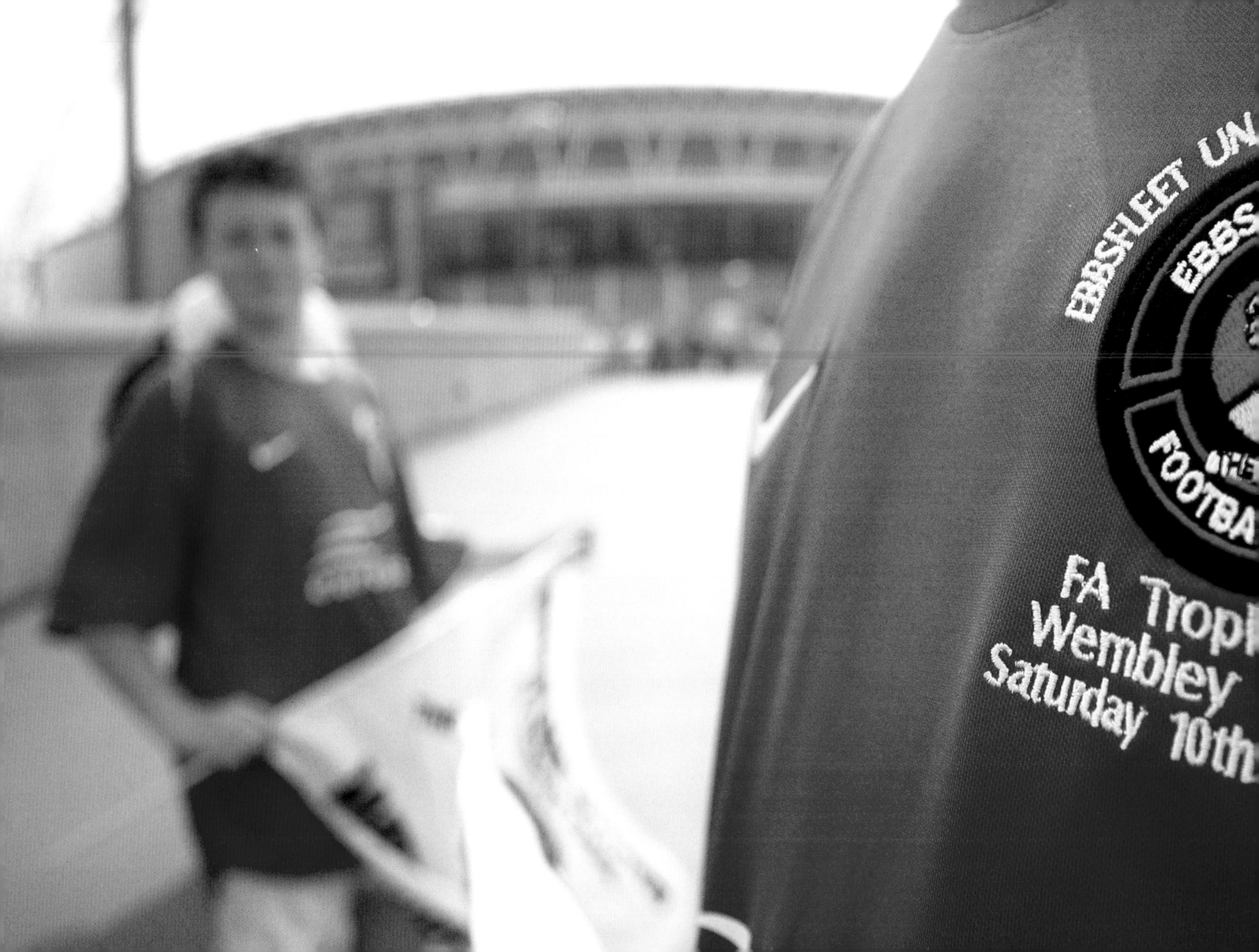
EBBSFLEET
FA
Wembley
Saturday

CHAPTER 3

NON-LEAGUE
GRACES THE
BIG STAGE

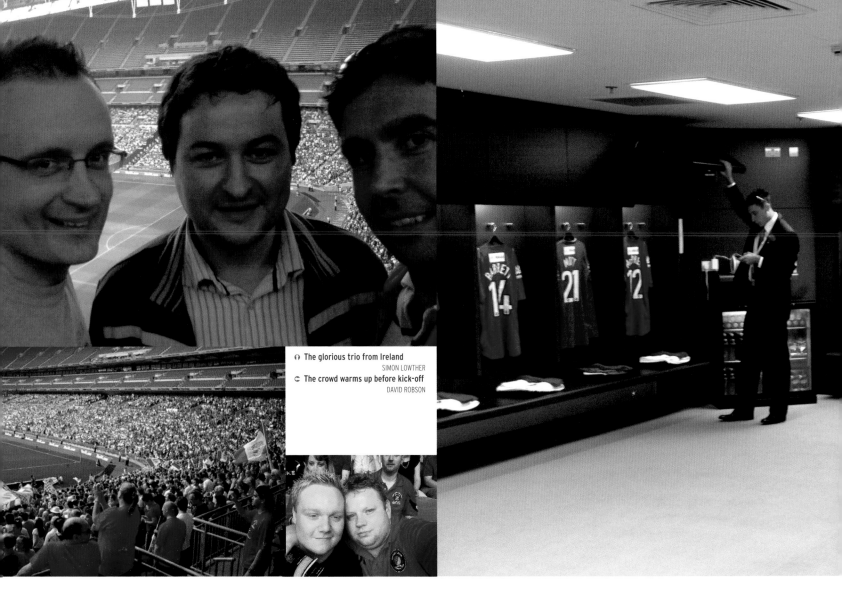

The glorious trio from Ireland
SIMON LOWTHER
The crowd warms up before kick-off
DAVID ROBSON

Non league football matches and 40,000 attendances in large stylish and all seater stadia are a couple of phrases that rarely meet and yet, on May 10 2008, this is precisely what happened. It is wonderful that the FA provides the opportunity for such a fabulous celebration of Conference level football.

As I watched a gathering of the clans making their way up Wembley way on an appropriately bright and sunny day, I felt a huge sense of pride, not just for our team, Ebbsfleet United, but also for our level of football in general. Far more, of course, needs to be done if football is going to continue to develop at all levels in this country but it was an acknowledgement that non league football really does matter and the numbers attending bore witness to this. For the regular fans that show up week after week it was a great reward for their dedication and a memory that they will cherish forever. For those whose attendance was a one-off, it was a reminder that non league football is vibrant and if only a small number of them become regular fans then the occasion will have been worth it for this alone

I can only imagine how fantastic it must have been for the players themselves. Although they are now professionals, football is for them something that they largely do just for the sheer enjoyment of the game. The financial rewards are relatively small and yet their effort, week after week, is not diminished and it is clear that they truly are the heart and soul of football in this country. Many of those who played in the final have never played in front of crowds of 10,000, let alone 40,000 in a stadium that is the showcase of the nation, yet on the pitch it was business as usual. No one appeared overawed and all rose to the occasion. Football, after all, is what they do.

It is quite possible, and indeed hopeful, that the Wembley occasion will bring non league football to the attention of many who would otherwise not be exposed to it. For me, however, the introduction to lower league football came much earlier in the season; indeed, well before it first became clear that Ebbsfleet would be the team that MyFootballClub would purchase.

My first game in fact was back in September 2007 at Accrington Stanley who were playing Grimsby Town. At the time, Accrington were seen as a distinct possibility for purchase having being reborn after financial problems had earlier caused their demise. They had successfully regained promotion to the league which was testament to what could be achieved with very little other than enthusiasm for the game. It was here that I met the first of my fellow MyFC members and it was at this moment that the whole venture became real. The football was less skilful than I was used to and certainly more frenetic. Nevertheless, it was a style of football that was far more enjoyable and it was very easy to quickly get engaged with it.

More matches quickly followed and pretty soon I was hooked. My first Ebbsfleet game was in »

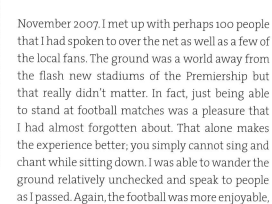

November 2007. I met up with perhaps 100 people that I had spoken to over the net as well as a few of the local fans. The ground was a world away from the flash new stadiums of the Premiership but that really didn't matter. In fact, just being able to stand at football matches was a pleasure that I had almost forgotten about. That alone makes the experience better; you simply cannot sing and chant while sitting down. I was able to wander the ground relatively unchecked and speak to people as I passed. Again, the football was more enjoyable, more engaging and I felt like I had reconnected once again with what the game was all about.

During the course of the season, I have now been to many games both home and away and have rarely been disappointed either by the football or the company. The reception has been almost universally friendly, opposing fans mix amiably in the bars and clubs and the banter remains friendly. While there is rivalry, of course, I think that all fans recognise what we have in common more than what divides us. I have met and talked with the coach, the directors of the club and the players, unthinkable at higher levels »

of football where such individuals are remote, ridiculously overpaid and a million miles away from grass roots football. The fans, players and officials involved in Premiership football should realise that without the lower leagues and their more friendly and informal nature, then the soul of football will quickly die and the big money of higher levels of football will go with it.

If you went to Wembley and got caught up in the experience and excitement of it, please consider getting involved in the bread and butter games, home or away. I will be surprised if you don't quickly get totally engaged with it. You will meet many new friends and get a real insight into what football is really about. The occasions will not be so grand or the facilities so lush. There will be lows to endure as well as highs to enjoy. However, if you do so and next year we are fortunate enough to feature at Wembley once again, either in the FA Trophy or in the Conference play-off finals, then you will not only enjoy the occasion all the more but will experience a sense of pride that you have been there from beginning to end. ⚽

PAUL CHARNOCK – Arithon

◖ **Alfie at his first ever football match, and what a match.** CHRIS MAW
◗ **Maxinho in the red seats!** LORRAINE HANDLEY

CHAPTER 4
EBBSWHAT?

EET UNITED FOOTBALL CLUB
HE FLEET
ROPHY FINAL - MAY 10 2008 - WEMBLEY

The woman at the Border Agency looked at us quizzically. You could tell that because of her petite build, she tried to exude strength and authority. But right now, strength and authority weren't on her mind. The two odd Americans in front of her were. Andrew, my buddy from Boston, and I had just disembarked from our transatlantic flight and had made our way to the front of the UK border control queue at Heathrow's Terminal 4. The usual questioning for any new arrival had taken a different path once the woman asked us why we were in Britain. "So this is American football?" "No," I said, "the football you know. But I can call it soccer if that helps." "Oh no, don't do that! But what is the club again and why are you here for them?" "It's Ebbsfleet United, the pride of Kent," I added a bit cheekily, as Andrew nodded solemnly next to me. "They're in the FA Trophy Final and we couldn't pass up a chance to see our club at Wembley." "And how did you two get to know about them?" "Well, you see, there's this website called MyFootballClub.co.uk, and it raised funds through memberships to buy a football club, and Ebbsfleet was the lucky club. We signed up for the website and now we're Fleet fans." Another of Andrew's solemn nods seconded this as well. The woman now looked completely baffled. "So had you ever been to, uh, Ebbsfleet to see them before this website bought the club?" "They actually play in Northfleet, only about 25 miles from London, and I don't think either of us had ever heard of

Ebbsfleet United before they got involved with MyFootballClub." Andrew echoed this statement by shaking his head. "Then how could you support them now?" Her incredulity was plain to see. "Football, our soccer, is a kids sport and only on the fringe of people's consciousness at home. But we knew about English football, even in the US, and we knew the passion of English football fans, and we wanted to be a part of it somehow." This merited a vigorous nod from Andrew. I continued, ❯❯

○ **Four guys and Mo!**   GARY ROZANSKI
↻ ↺ **Robert and Julie, Dylan and Luke Walker**
ROBERT WALKER
○ **Party at Stonebridge Road on the day before the big game**
↻ **Steve, Graham and the Americans at Stonebridge Road**

NATHAN HENDLER

"But it seemed fake to one day stand up and claim, 'today I support Liverpool,' or Man U or whoever. There'd be no connection with the club and its established supporters could rightfully wonder where we got off saying we were fans of their club. But then MyFootballClub came along and gave us Americans the chance to get in on the ground floor of something, to be a part of something real, to have a real relationship with an English football club and its fans."

By now, the queue had started backing up and, realising that we had no ill intent, even if we were out of the ordinary, she shook her head lightly, stamped our passports and wished us a good stay, although the last was with a bit of a smirk. The next time I saw such a smirk was at Wembley. Already several brews to the good, Andrew and I met up with another MyFootballClub member from Massachusetts, Max, and headed to the stadium. Once there, we bumped into a guy who looked more outfitted for the yacht club than watching a football club. But he was nice enough and we got to chatting before the game. He noticed the shirt I was wearing. "Mister Ham Man? What's that, the sponsor of an old Fleet kit?" From 1994," I said, beaming at him proudly. "There's nothing eBay can't do!" He shook his head and chuckled, and talked about how surprised he was to see so many people from outside of Kent at the match. The three of us extolled the virtues of MyFC and lauded how it had connected us with the Fleet.

"Too bad you can't vote for me," he said with a wry sort of smile and that's when we understood we had been shooting the breeze »

⟳ **MyFootballClubs: Ebbsfleet United and sc Heerenveen at Wembley!** JELMER BOOTS
⤴ **The team lining up for the national anthem** ROBERT BOYCE
⤵ **Our first real live look at Ebbsfleet's players during the pre-match warmup**
EUGENE KING-HAUGHEY
⤴ **On the big screen above the yellow hoardes, all set to come out in front of the biggest crowd of their careers** NICK FISK

The excitement
builds and flags
begin to wave
before kick-off
JELMER BOOTS

with Gravesham's Member of Parliament.

Saw a grin of this type leaving England, too, when we were back at Heathrow the next day, after the Fleet's stirring victory. We were being interrogated again, this time by an American who acted like he worked for the Department of Homeland Security and looked us over with grim determination. His frown turned upside down, however, when we told him we had come over to watch football. It turns out that John from Buffalo was a closet soccer fanatic and that his posting to England had allowed him to indulge his enthusiasm for the game. When we discovered he supported Arsenal, we sprung into action: "You need to look into MyFootballClub and Ebbsfleet," Andrew and I both implored, "because you need a real club, a non league club, to support!". "Not non league for long if what you guys say is true," he rightfully retorted. He then sent us down the jet way, smiling behind us. It wasn't until I got settled in my seat did I see the MyFC/Fleet bookmark stuck into my in-flight reading. I called over the gate attendant, who had luckily been on the plane checking that all was in readiness for departure, handed her the bookmark and asked if she'd give it to John. She nodded and looked at me quizzically but took the bookmark with her. I'd like to believe MyFootballClub has a new member and the Fleet a new fan from that bookmark.

Amongst all the run-ins with people confused or bemused, the Americans and Canadians who came over for the FA Trophy Final were treated like family by the long time supporters of Ebbsfleet United; like an eccentric uncle from across the pond, perhaps, but like family nevertheless. And that makes us proud to be fans of the Fleet, as much so as the score line of the match, and we thank the local supporters for welcoming us and making us feel like we have a second home in Kent. ⚽

JOSH FRIEDMAN – Friejose

CHAPTER 5

NORTHERNERS
ON TOUR

⚲ **Alfie Westhead poses while The Fleet battle on**   DAVID WESTHEAD

'm sat in a pub in London, a stone's throw away from the intimidating News International building known as 'Fortress Murdoch', around a table populated mostly by Sun newspaper employees who have all sat down to enjoy a well-earned pint after a long shift. It's a modern identikit pub situated on the ground floor of a large concrete building opposite the newspaper offices. On initial reflection, it feels like being in a scene straight from the memoirs of former newspaper editor Piers Morgan, except much less glamorous and infinitely less smug. Feeling underdressed, as everyone else is 'smart-casual' straight from the office, and socially awkward amongst strangers, I try and quell the slight paranoia that I'm getting funny looks due to being the only person to order a pint of bitter.

Not all of the faces are unfamiliar; perched uncomfortably on a stool to the right of me is the towering, yet gangly, frame of my travelling companion, long-time friend and fellow MyFC owner Colin Taylor (colcake). Three of the others belong to friends I graduated from university with, one of which, Mark, is the reason that this trip has been possible in the first place. The offer of free accommodation and first class grub (two living room sofas and a curry) in our nation's pricey capital was too good to turn down, especially since we had little change left from the extortionate train fare.

The journey to London was not without its problems – we missed our pre-booked seats on the 16.52 from Preston to Euston by a matter of seconds. Arriving on the platform, sans-dignity, after legging it through the city centre from being dropped off in a traffic jam, we discovered we had been stood on the wrong platform as our actual train left without us. After some red-face wrangling with customer services, our tickets were eventually validated for the next available train, which was to embark only half an hour later.

The train journey itself was as pleasant as public transport can be; Colin eagerly leafed through the pages of his freshly-purchased FHM, voicing both his agreement and disapproval over the rankings of the latest 'Top 100 Sexiest Women', whilst I set to work on the few cans of bitter I'd stowed away underneath the table.

Finally alighting at Euston, we successfully circumnavigated the underground to Tower Hill, where I promptly got us lost. Even more embarrassing for me, the route from the tube station to 'Fortress Murdoch' was one I'd made several times before after spending a fortnight on placement there only two years earlier. One wrong turn in St Katherine's Dock in the dark added an extra 45 sweaty minutes on to our walk to meet Mark and his colleagues in the pub.

As we sat and supped our pints around the large table by the window, faces came and went. Mark had to make several introductions throughout the evening, pleasantries were exchanged and hands were shaken but, shamefully, I don't remember a ⟫

○ **The Fleet prepare to defend a Torquay free kick**   DAVID ROBSON

single name. "So what are you in London for?" they would ask. "We're going to Wembley", I enthusiastically replied, eliciting a genuine look of interest and curiosity on the faces of The Sun employees. "Oh! Who's playing?" would come next. "Ebbsfleet United and Torquay United in the FA Trophy Final," I stated proudly. "Oh ...".

Over the course of our evening in the pub, my reply received reactions ranging from confusion to mild derision and would often incur an awkward silence until someone piped up to explain that it was non league cup football and Ebbsfleet were that team that had been bought out by a group of internet fans. A low murmur of feigned interest would pass and then the topic would swiftly change.

The rest of the night passed us by in a speedy blur. The curry we were promised never happened and was instead replaced with more beer. We caught a train back to Mark's, failing to take any notice of where we were or where we were going but enjoyed watching as he failed to charm two travelling Canadian girls back to his house.

We awoke the next morning, grubby, sore- ➤➤

headed and with no clue where we were, just in time to hear Mark utter something about being "well late" as he left for work. We stumbled from the house into the sunshine and miraculously found our way from Borehamwood all the way to Wembley Stadium, the first glimpse of which I saw from the train; the stadium's huge white arch curving through the bright blue London skyline.

As we took our seats, I thought back to the conversations in the pub the night before. I could just about understand the lack of enthusiasm over non league cup football, especially about a team no-one outside of Kent has ever heard of. I wasn't bothered by the notion that these people may have thought we were mental for travelling all this way and paying to watch it. In fact, it is a thought that had crossed my mind several times already that day when running for the train or going cross-eyed over a map of the underground.

Twelve months previously, MyFC had been a pipe dream that I'd taken up on a whim. But now, sat amongst 25,000 other singing dreamers all bathed in swathes of red and white under the sweeping arch at the redeveloped 'home of football', I knew why I'd joined in the first place. In a time where the Premier League is more concerned with money and celebrity than the game itself, Ebbsfleet United and MyFC have just started out on a new path where the fans truly come first because they are nurturing their own club, not being treated as a cash-cow by some billionaire foreign owner.

To make it to any Wembley final means you've made football history. To see the Fleet, a club I've grown to know in only a few short months and now love as my own, lift the trophy in front of me and their 25,000 other fans means I've lived it. ⚽

DOM SANNA – (dj54nna)

⮌ Zarita and Stonz from Norway enjoying a fantastic day at Wembley with their young Ebbsfleet United fans!
KENNETH DALHAUGH

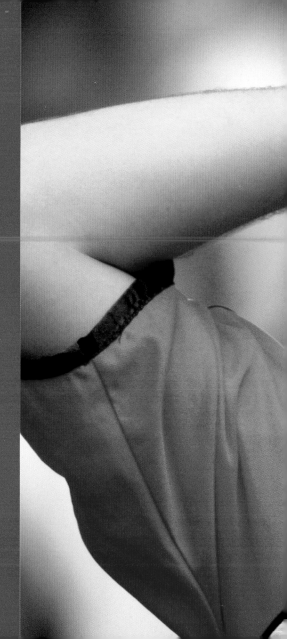

CHAPTER 6

JOURNALIST
GLORY HUNTER

At 2:30pm on May 10 2008, I was somewhere completely and utterly different to where I expected to be, or really deserved to be. Three hundred feet high in the new Wembley Stadium, cheering on a team that I didn't just own but supported, accompanied by 25,000 likeminded Ebbsfleet United fans. As far a cry from my typical weekends as you could get.

A usual Saturday afternoon for me used to be, strangely at 2.30 pm, pegging it home after an early shift in work for an afternoon in the company of Jeff Stelling and his Sky Sports News posse accompanied by a selection of Greggs finest pasties and pastries and a handful of football coupons. Since then, I had upgraded my weekends to actually writing about football, at a local and amateur level. I get the joys of reliving the damp and dreary weekends of my youth around Edinburgh's local council playing fields where most matches are mud skewed or called off due to the weather before the weekend even starts!

At the 'business end' of the season, the organisations from all competition levels and age groups can cram all their hopes, dreams and potential into one glorious cup final. During these occasions it's truly an honour to walk through the gates (and not have to pay the £2 entrance fee!) and be part of something special for all concerned even though it's not something that I can share on the same level as everyone else involved. At least I can walk around in front of the barrier that keeps the eager spectators pinned back yards from infringing on the pitch. It's not quite a press box but it's better than nothing!

But even at the 'business end' of the season, where there is so much to report on and so little space to cram it all in I couldn't resist making the journey from Scotland's capital to England's capital in order to be part of something I truly didn't really deserve. Ebbsfleet United were barely a blip in my lower league knowledge when I'd watched ≫

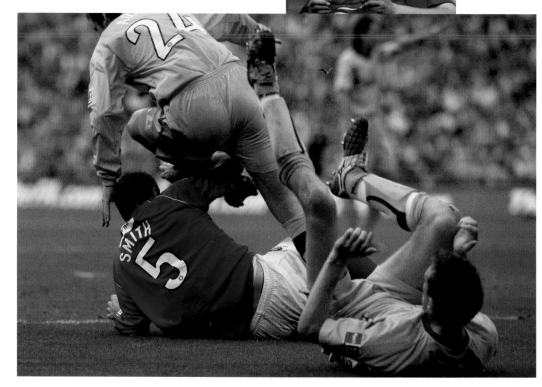

the first ever final at the new Wembley on TV. Not even when I had the opportunity to stroll around the stadium on FA Cup Final day in 2007 would I have believed for a second I would truly be able to support a team as much as I supported Ebbsfleet on 10 May 2008.

My usual journey to most games around Edinburgh is a bus ride away, with a five minute walk off the beaten track to the most remote pitches. My journey to Wembley consisted of an hour on the bus, half an hour on the airport bus, two hours in the airport, over an hour flying down, half an hour on the train into Victoria and three tube interchanges; then all reversed eight hours later. Total cost over £100, a bit more than the usual £1 bus fare in Edinburgh!

It was the walk down Wembley Way which proved to be the shortest journey of all but undoubtedly the most memorable. I was surrounded by fans, some of whom would have been to see Ebbsfleet at Stonebridge Road hundreds of times whilst some My Football Club members would have spent thousands travelling from all around the globe to join the throng for the FA Trophy Final. It was ducking under the Wembley Arch when something snapped in my head. This wasn't just a jaunt to see any team play any competitive game. It wasn't the chance to even see a team that I support play. It was the chance to cheer a team in which I have a financial input and democratic decisions to make playing at Wembley in a cup final! My usual Saturday afternoon's football involves doing a few laps of a muddy pitch and occasionally having to kick the ball back for a throw in or stop it invading the adjacent match.
»

At Wembley, I was seated in Block 550 (yes, 'the nosebleeds') back at row 34. No chance of getting a touch of the ball up there, sadly. Like the majority of 'first timers' to an Ebbsfleet game, I had kept informed of the team and performances through the wealth of information in podcasts, streams and discussion within the MyFC crew. This bubbling social network also leads to being informed of the cult worshipping of Sacha Opinel and unrelated mystique of 'The Red Toothbrush'. All of this was swirling around my head at the altitude where I was less watching Torquay United swirl balls from back to front with ease in the opening period but drinking in the atmosphere and occasion of a truly unique Trophy Final.

When I had finally snapped out of daydreaming in the humid heights, Ebbsfleet began to assert themselves on the proceedings and I fought hard to restrain myself and I took out the notepad and started knitting together a match report. But the football itself seemed somewhat incidental to the game, the actual 90 minutes were barely considered. The Fleet were going to walk away with the FA Trophy, no other outcome made sense. But when Chris McPhee's penalty was saved everything began to swirl; surely The Fleet couldn't lose? It wasn't in the script! I had distanced myself from much of the balanced build up, although we were clear underdogs on paper. However, this was a paper that 25,000 red shirted fans doing the Mexican Wave a few minutes later weren't subscribing to.

There's always a hero, a workhorse, an unselfish and sometimes unheralded starlet in every team. From Sunday league to Champions League, every game balances the glory getter with provider and the imposing John Akinde duly provided for McPhee to grab the glory and atone for his error moments before half time. The goal proved to be the only one of the game and came from the sheer belief of Akinde to hound a ball bound for a goal kick, a slice of luck that it rebounded into his path and fantastic vision to line up McPhee. The same belief Akinde had displayed was passed around the Ebbsfleet fans weeks ahead of the fixture, days before travelling and right up to the stroll walk up Wembley Way. Although Torquay came close to equalising on a few occasions, it seemed written that we would be able to hang on. Once the Mexican wave halted at the blue and yellow end of the fantastic stadium, you could see the difference in the support. 25,000 fans, probably at least half of which had boarded the red and white internet bandwagon, were sending waves of encouragement and optimism to their eleven men on the pitch whilst an end of the ground filled with life long fans seemed to have accepted their fate. Even the empty middle tier of 16,932 corporate seats was dressed in red! And when Stacey Long cleared off the line the balance of support in those seats around the stadium refused to shift – the trophy wasn't going anywhere but Stonebridge Road. ⚽

NIALL McNEILL – Perfect Darkness

⚘ **The best fans in the world!**   MATTHEW PEARCE

CHAPTER 7
PRAWN SANDWICH, ANYONE?

Prawn sandwich, anyone? This is the ultimate insult to any self-respecting football supporter. Ever since Roy Keane's infamous outburst, to be labelled a member of the 'prawn sandwich brigade' has become synonymous with fans who know more about a good cabernet sauvignon than a centre-back, and probably think the Christmas tree formation is all about making the fairy lights look pretty in December.

It was therefore with some trepidation that we swallowed our pride along with a fruity little red and signed up for Ebbsfleet United's hospitality package for the FA Trophy Final at Wembley. We had already sampled the pie and locally brewed pint at Burton Albion in the quarter-final. Now, like our team, we were about to enjoy a special experience on a very special day. With great excitement and anticipation we joined the throng of Fleet fans in the heat and bustle of Wembley Way, before entering the less frenetic splendour of the stadium's air-conditioned Corinthian Suite.

The seats of Wembley Stadium glowed red through the smoked glass windows; a good omen for the Fleet who play in that colour. Our table was a microcosm of how Ebbsfleet United has changed and evolved this season with its acquisition by MyFootballClub Supporters, as on all the other tables and, indeed, seats in the ground, were from across the world: Europe, America, Australia, and even Chesterfield. We may have spoken with a mixture of accents but everyone was ready to shout his or her loudest for the Fleet.

Naturally, we had to ensure that our throats »

EBBSFLEET
GOALSCORER

12

CHRIS
MCPHEE

were well lubricated for the singing and chanting ahead. Our plates were piled high with typical footballing fare like smoked salmon, couscous and the inevitable prawns when a horrified silence momentarily descended as someone declared the wine to be 'blended'. Once the shock of that revelation had worn off, however, the burning questions had still to be debated: would Liam play 4-3-3 or 4-4-2? Would Chukki be preferred up front to Luke? Would Sacha manage 90 minutes without being shown a yellow card? The talk was entirely about football from then on. Although we all felt like guests at a wedding reception, we knew the ceremony was still to some.

The first sight of the Wembley pitch is still, even without its iconic Twin Towers, enough to bring a lump to every throat. The sense of occasion

was finally beginning to do what it always does at a football match – hearts were beating faster, hands were shaking (and not from the alcohol), and suddenly there was an immense tension and anticipation of the drama to come. Was it so different in the corporate seats? It is true that they are wide, padded, very comfortable and have a fabulous view. Yet, as we all joined lustily in singing the National Anthem, we realised that the atmosphere and passion and sheer desire to see our team play well and win, was just the same as if we had been standing on the humblest piece of terracing in the Blue Square Premier.

Scientists may argue that time passes at the same pace whatever one is doing. They are obviously not football supporters. The first half seemed to go quicker than Stacy down the left- »

⊕ **Rezthered celebrates McPhee's goal from up high**   MARK BAILEY

wing, as the Fleet rear guard defiantly repelled a determined Torquay side which had failed to reach the play-offs and so had everything to prove – and win – in the Trophy Final. For 25 minutes, the tension was palpable as Torquay looked sharp and threatening. Then the miracle happened; the Fleet were awarded a penalty. Ex-Torquay striker Chris McPhee had not missed one of his previous five. He stepped up, and to almost tangible disbelief, the Torquay keeper made a memorable save.

Galvanised by this, Ebbsfleet seemed to find fresh inspiration all over the pitch. Big John, the unofficial Man of the Match, epitomised the Fleet spirit by never knowing when he was beaten. In the forty-fifth minute he harried and chased down a ball which should never have been his and his inch-perfect cross found Chris who calmly stroked the ball into the back of the net. That certainly changed Liam's half-time team talk!

It changed ours too. We were now one-nil up and the tension was not just about finishing our drinks before half-time was up. There was a genuine sense of theatre as we took our seats for the second half (although nobody dared to shout: 'break a leg'!). Exacerbated by rumbling thunder and a flash of lightning, the atmosphere was electric in more ways than one. Songs and chants echoed all around the Ebbsfleet section of the ground (no, we did not sing 'who ate all the prawns' in the hospitality seats), and we all joined in enthusiastically with the Mexican Wave. Torquay fans, for some reason, did not want to participate in that!

The second half saw a magnificent display by the Fleet and we will never forget Big John's towering and mature performance, Lance's crucial saves, Chris's dedication of his goal to his ill sister, and, yes, a gung-ho tackle by Sacha that was nonetheless timed to perfection and which elicited one of the biggest roars of the day from the Fleet fans. When, deep into the second half, Elliot Benyon missed a header for Torquay that his grandmother could probably have converted, we just knew the day would belong to Ebbsfleet. And as referee Martin Atkinson blew the final whistle, gloriously it did.

We cheered and clapped and shouted ourselves hoarse to see Paul lift the silver Trophy aloft, and what a great captain he is to share that moment with the unfortunate, injured Danny. Somehow we forgot our pre-match declaration that just getting to Wembley was enough; it was the occasion that mattered and not necessarily the winning. The winning – typified by the grin on Liam's face that was wider than the Wembley arch; the sheer delight of every Fleet fan, old and new, all around us; the throats that could sing and chant no more – was very much about joy and achievement and glory and jubilation, thank you very much! The dream had come true.

Oh, and crossing the Roy Keane line from a pie and a pint to prawns and white wine, it didn't hurt a bit! ⊛

JIM & JANE WRIGHT – Jimboman

Fans celebrating
at the end of the
first half, just after
McPhee's goal
KEVIN BUTTON

CHAPTER 8

LINFIELD
KEEPER'S
TROPHY
FINAL DAY

May 10 2008, a day none of us will soon forget. Thousands of people from all across the globe came together at the hallowed hall of football to drive their beloved football club to the highest of heights in our first ever FA Trophy final. We all played different roles in helping this dream to come true and the following is my little part in this matter.

My name is Willie Groshell. I am a proud letter carrier for the USPS. I work in the city of Newberg, Oregon, population just over 21,000, and I live in the nearby city of McMinnville. The second Saturday in May is our nationwide annual letter carrier food drive for the hungry where we not only complete our usual appointed rounds but we collect donations of non-perishable foods which we then deliver to our local food banks all around the USA. Last year all across the USA we collected 70.7 million pounds of food. Needless to say, this May 10 was a very busy day indeed.

I set my alarm an extra half hour early for Saturday morning but that didn't matter, I was so anxious and excited that I awoke on my own a half hour before my alarm. It was 4:45am, I hit the bathroom to get ready for the day and 15 minutes later I was in my uniform (plus my FA Trophy semi-final pin I got from the Fleet shop secured on my lapel, not regulation but small enough to keep from getting into any trouble at work) and more or less ready. My lovely wife is sleeping peacefully so all that I do in the morning is kept quiet out of respect. As soon as I leave the bedroom and bathroom, I turn the computer on to catch up with whatever live feeds I can from the internet to help with the build-up before kick-off. A quick breakfast, a cup of tea (and two more ready for the road in my thermal cups) and I take my place in front of my monitor, the sound is turned off (sleeping missus, remember) and I begin to receive some of the images from Wembley and the surrounding grounds. How sweet the anticipation, my heart »

beat quickens and the energy builds. The stands, packed with red, so many faithful Fleet fans old and new... the pitch, perfect and the energy builds. At last, we see the players enter the pitch, the moment is near, the crowd is electric, at last the game is nearly afoot and we will know who deserves to raise the FA Trophy this year. All this time I have been attempting to save the live video stream from the webcast (it failed somehow) and just as the teams take their respective positions on the pitch to begin the game, I have to leave home so I will not be late to work. I am placed into football limbo and, to make matters worse, I forgot to charge my cell phone the night before so it dies shortly after I leave my home for work.

Imagine, if you will, the anxiety of knowing that one of the biggest, most meaningful football games of your life is happening right now and you have no way of being able to watch/listen or receive any reports for the next (due to a sick call or two and lots of overtime) 12 and a half hours. Anxiety and constant wondering were thick upon me this morning and throughout the day. In hindsight (from accounts of the match, I still haven't gotten to see the game) my feelings and actions reflected how our lads played that day. Driving to work, I was so anxious with wondering how the match was going that I felt unsettled but after the first 15 minutes or so I said to myself, "enough of this worrying, just believe and the lads will take care of the rest". So that is exactly what I did, I let out a nice loud, "Come On You Reds!" in the car and put on my resolve to stay positive and give the lads all the backing I possibly could from 5,000 miles away. Work was long, the day was cool and grey but it always feels good to be able »

♫ **Martin and Meg in a sea of red**
MARTIN THIRKETTLE
♫ **Miss YF with The Red Toothbrush**
LORRAINE HANDLEY

to do some work on behalf of those in need. At the end of the work day, we had collected 7 tons of food in the city of Newberg alone, I had delivered nearly two full postal routes of mail and the FA Trophy Final match had been over for hours and my lingering anxiety was still with me but it was put behind my overwhelming faith that our lads would do us proud like they have so many times before. All day, in my head, I repeated over and over, "Come On You Reds!" (not a good idea to say out loud while representing the USA during work). Once I made it home, I gave my missus a hug and a kiss then headed for the computer as I had to see the result that I had felt in my heart all day. I quickly went to MyFootballClub.co.uk and logged in to confirm what I felt and low and behold there was the proof, 1-0. The Fleet are victorious and our combined dreams have come true. My fellow fans have shared so many images and stories from this glorious day and as I watch, read and soak them in I continue to get a tingle up and down my spine and I can't seem to wipe this goofy smile off of my face. Thank you all for sharing this day with me and the rest of the world.

You might think that I had nothing to do with the match, that work kept me too busy and away from it all but if you do you are mistaken. You may not have seen me at Wembley, but my spirit was right there beside you cheering the whole game. You may not have heard me but my voice combined with yours and carried our lads to

victory. We have created something together that is much bigger than any of us could possibly be on our own. Human beings are social creatures, we all long for a place where we can "belong" and feel like a real vital and useful part of something important. We have created this very place and we have opened it to the rest of the world. Some people say that technology is destroying humanity and our connection with our fellow man but we are living proof that, when used properly, technology helps to bring people together and breaks down barriers between people of all nations. Our future is boundless and our joys will, hopefully, grow as we work together, moving forward and helping to place our football club as a model for the rest of the world to follow. Up the Fleet!!! The FA Trophy is ours!!! ⚽

WILLIE GROSHELL – Linfield Keeper

⊕ **The scarf raised high** PETER TAYLOR

CHAPTER 9

PRESS RECORD
BRIAN!

t all began the day after Ebbsfleet United won their semi-final match with Aldershot with a fairly tongue-in-cheek e-mail that said something along the lines of... "Hey all, the club that JC and I own (along with 28,998 other people!), Ebbsfleet United, won their FA Trophy semi-final on Saturday (4-2 over favourites Aldershot) and will be playing in the 'hugely prestigious' FA Trophy Final on 10 May at Wembley Stadium. As owners, JC and I feel obliged to see the team that we moulded into finalists attempt to lift the trophy. It's also a great chance to see the new Wembley Stadium and a cup final! Let me know if you fancy coming."

As the replies filtered back, I realised that I had assembled a fairly unlikely collection of football fans. Aside from me there was JC, an egg-chaser at heart but also a fellow MyFC member and his American/Danish fiancé Sanne (a football novice). Then there was Phil, another rugby fan but with an England shirt dutifully worn for all sports, and his German lawyer girlfriend Nic. Jezza, a Reading

FC season ticket holder, wanted to come too, as did my girlfriend, Sharon, who has only ever been to one football match in her life (Malaga vs. Osasuna in La Liga) and has never seen a live goal – Malaga-Osasuna ended 0-0.

May 10 finally rolled around and at the (very) last minute Sharon decided that she had to make a banner for the final. So, we quickly ran into the local newsagent and grabbed a red marker pen and a sheet of thick birthday wrapping paper with pink cakes on one side. Desperate times called for desperate measures! The quickly-scribbled banner just said the words "PRESS RECORD BRIAN!" Explanation? Sharon's dad is the aforementioned 'Brian' and he is also a member of MyFC. He is a huge football fan but unfortunately he suffers from Parkinson's disease and the one thing guaranteed to set it off is the one thing that he enjoys the most – sport! So, Brian would be at home watching on TV and Sharon was determined to get on TV so that he could see her and hopefully laugh at the banner – as well as ⟫

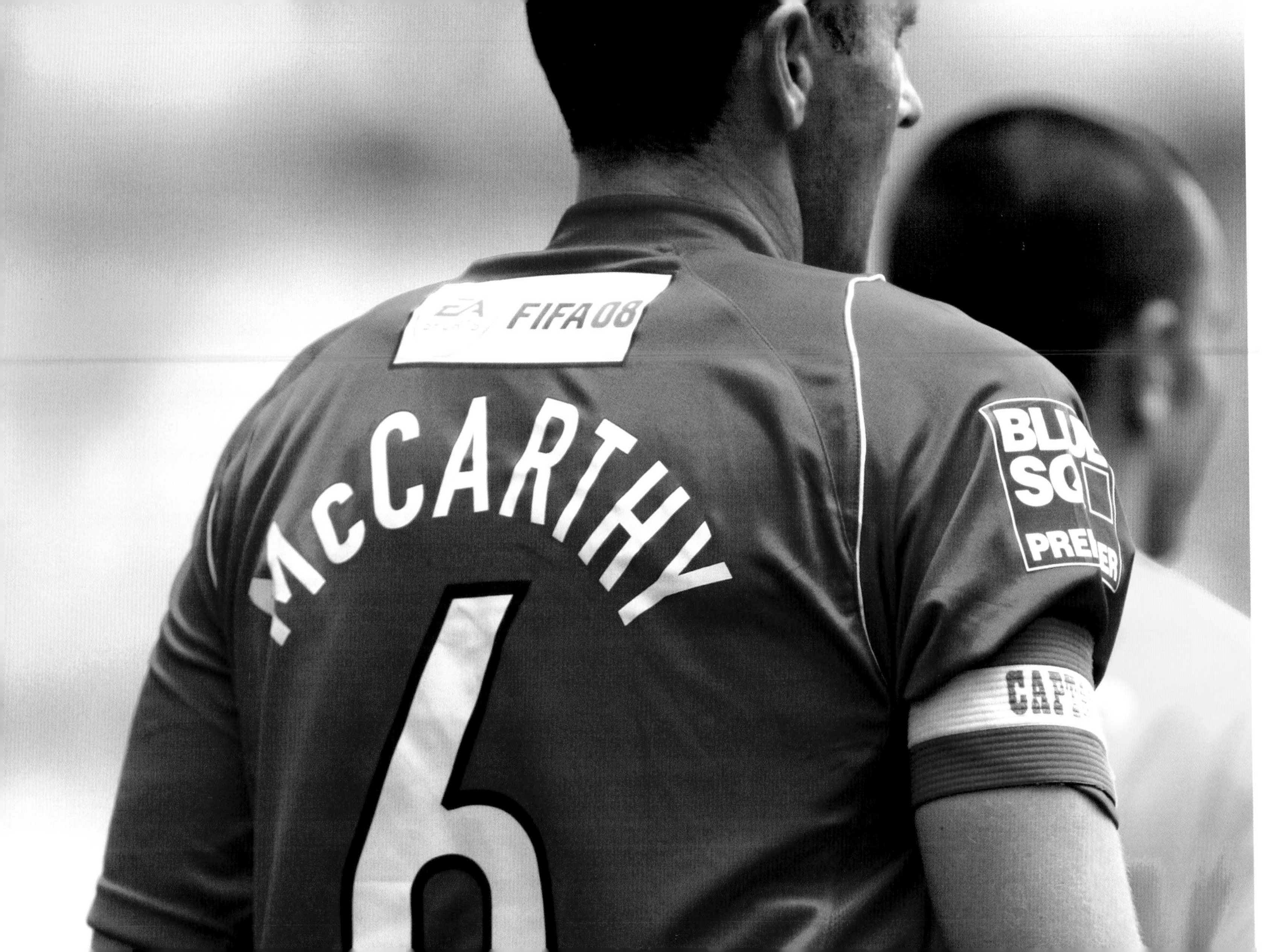

FIFA 08
McCARTHY
6

quite seriously reminding him to press record.

As for meeting up with my rag bag of newly converted Ebbsfleet fans, early signs were not good. Jez was late, Phil would be delayed and Nic was asking just how bad non league football was as she had only ever been to games in the Bundesliga and always sat in the press box.

As we finally got to Wembley Stadium, we became part of a constantly growing and often chanting mass of red and yellow shirts. This was definitely something new to some of my crowd and I could sense an apprehension in the air, despite the fans being in good spirits. As we started up the Bobby Moore Way, I was suddenly hit with a burst of excitement and anticipation for the game ahead. I miss the Twin Towers but this new stadium is an amazing structure. As we walked into Block 143, I realised just how close we were actually going to be to the pitch. The best reaction actually came from Phil who arrived late and just stood at the top of stairs looking around in awe and then said with a huge grin on his face: "Top seats mate! And I just saw my first ever football punch-up on the way in. This is brilliant." Rugby fans eh?!

As kick-off neared, JC and Sanne, originally in white, returned with a red Ebbsfleet United t-shirt and an England logo cap. JC explained that he just didn't feel right wearing white. It wasn't enough to watch this game; you had to become part of it. The cameras were now rolling and Sharon was permanently holding up her banner. She actually managed to get herself on the giant screens at either end of the pitch a number of times but we still don't know if she made it on to the TV coverage.

The game started and I always feel that you can see how football affects people by their reaction during the first contentious incident. Cronin's early saves wouldn't provide that contention but then Stacey Long hammered a shot that forced Martin Rice to dive spectacularly across his goal. He was beaten but the ball flew just wide. The crowd all stood as one and a giant "ohhhh" erupted from the »

🎧 **Fever pitch...** SIMON LOWTHER

red end of the ground followed by heavy applause. All of my friends had stood as one and were now clapping. Even the guys that had never been in a football crowd before joined in. Nic, Phil and Jez were laughing along with the loud fan wearing a women's top, swearing his head off and showing his arse. Sharon was explaining her banner to strangers all around us and I was engrossed in the game and the running commentary I was getting from the old boys in the seats behind.

As half time neared, Luke Moore broke into the box and was fouled and an almighty cheer went

up as the penalty was awarded. The celebration confused Sharon who cheered and then said "I didn't even see the ball go in". As Chris McPhee stepped up to take the penalty someone behind me said "He hasn't missed one all season". This was followed by Sharon reminding me that "she hadn't ever seen a live goal". McPhee's shot was saved and I began to wonder if Sharon was some sort of jinx. Nic didn't help by quietly asking if anyone in England can actually take a penalty properly.

It was all okay a couple of minutes later though when, following some great work by John Akinde, McPhee bundled in to make amends and give the Fleet the lead and Sharon had finally seen her first live goal. Everyone was in an even bigger football frame of mind for the second half, although I must admit that passing around Haribo Star Mix was a first for me, and when the final whistle went the echo of fans' whistles suddenly changed to cheering and applause that continued for what seemed like hours.

We slowly exited the ground and as we walked down towards Wembley Park Tube everyone was saying what a top day that they had. I even heard Nic ask Phil if he would take her to another game soon and we all decided to go for a kick-about in the park back home. I wouldn't say that they were all converts exactly but, for a couple of hours on a sunny Saturday in May, Wembley and Ebbsfleet United had turned them into fans. ⚽

JAMES COULBAULT – Regis04

⊃ Cheer up,
the Fleet are
one-nil up!
CULLEN HENSHAW

CHAPTER 10

A TARTAN EBBSFLEET DIARY

May 10 2008

Wow! It's 4.00am, the chat the night before and into the early hours had been about who might be there and what might happen. The MyFC party at the Wembley Sports Club was a certainty, whilst the ever present discussion about the airline being used was probably tempting fate... if only we'd known. The week leading up to the final had almost been as interesting as the FA Trophy run itself but it was now time to look past the conversations at work and the "Ebbswho?" We were heading for Wembley, 20,000 plus and in only six hours I'd be among them. The car will arrive soon, Mark and George both flying down with me, and they'll appear at the party later.

It's getting close to 8.00am and we've just landed. I'd actually forgotten my passport and we had to go back to pick it up. I'm sitting in Costa Coffee, having met up with Felix (FNEX) and we're wondering if Doheochai and Coocumber will show up. I have yet to actually be outside for very long and it's going to be a train and then a tube before I can feel the sunshine.

10.00am and, sat in the MyFC pre-match party, I've just about recovered from the initial blast of heat as I exited Wembley Park Station and the initial impression of the Stadium is fresh in my mind. I'm one of the first four into the venue, holding up the Scottish custom of being at the bar before it's even open. The other MyFC members start filtering in: Staff, Canagoon, Arithon, Shooter,

the Foxes and then around half of Manchester including Weenie, Markrowly and Ockers. The debate of switching to shorts has already begun, the St. Mirren shorts in my bag just waiting the right moment.

1.00pm and I quite literally can't, or is that cannae, believe the range of Nationalities represented at this party. I've either walked over to or been approached by people from the UK, Finland, Germany, Australia, Canada, USA, Italy, Turkey and Spain to name just a few. It's exactly what MyFC should be about and it's a shame we all have a match to go to. Like all good Scots on holiday, I also now have my money and ticket tucked into my socks. One last thing to do before ≫

⟰ **Manicscot, The Praying Scot** KEITH A. HANDLEY
⟰ **Flashmeister departs Inverness, Scotland** FLASHMEISTER

heading to the match itself and that was to be interviewed for the podcast. My interview didn't appear in the final release but Flashmeister more than deserves to represent Scotland on that front.

Weeeeeeeeeeeeeeeeeeeeeeeeembley!!!! Yes, it's there in all its glory and I can honestly say that it looks absolutely phenomenal. Again, MyFC members from all over the globe are saying hello as we walk along Olympic Way. We stop to take a picture. I believe it actually appeared in the Non League newspaper and I have a chance to look back at what seems a never-ending red sea. There's the occasional dot of yellow including Howezy and merchandise sellers, but it does look at that point as if Ebbsfleet United have taken over. All we need to do now is find the entrance and make our way into the ground itself, a brief nod towards Bobby Moore's statue the only break.

2.00pm and we're inside. It's time to meet or be around even more MyFC members. Bigislander, Butski, Katiegsteele, Gadgetman and so many others whose names escape me. The surreal feeling hits me, a realisation that I'm the co-owner of a club playing at Wembley and I briefly wonder if there have been even 1,000 other people who could have said the same whilst standing here before today. The teams are read out and it's fairly similar to the side Felix and I discussed on the train to Liverpool Street. McCarthy has come in for Hawkins, with Hawkins in turn moving across to replace Ricketts. The customary pleasantries are observed with the team being introduced to someone and the National Anthem playing, there was also the comical addition of a few people nudging me and saying "come on Kenny, you know the words!". I also began to suffer due to the ≫

♫ **Celebrating at the final whistle** JOHN HORVATH

♫ **Archie gives a cheer for The Fleet** JIM LOCKWOOD

heat and my eyes, I get weeping eyes occasionally, and this only added to the whole comedy effect of the moment.

The match itself is mainly a blur. I'd be lying if I said I can recall everything without watching it back on tape. It was no surprise that Torquay came out all guns blazing whilst some of the Ebbsfleet players looked like a newly born calf trying to find its legs. Thankfully, things settled down and the early scares passed. The players appeared to be lifted by the crowd and the occasion as we played more football than I've seen us do for a while and the latter part of the first half was all Ebbsfleet; Opinel and Bostwick, for example, both having fine efforts on goal. Then, it happened, we were awarded a penalty and up stepped Chris McPhee… the man I've been scouting for the MyFC Scouting group. He missed, but I felt it was a great save and we just hoped it wasn't the last chance we'd get as we sat back down dejected. Minutes later the ball comes to Opinel and he hammers it forward. I'm still complaining about the pass when Markhere nudges me and Yorkfox grabs my wrist. I look up and Akinde has just robbed the Torquay defender, I look across and there's my man McPhee racing in "PASS IT, PASS IT…GOOOOOOAAALLL!!!!!!!!!!" Ebbsfleet United go one-nil up and Wembley Stadium absolutely erupts. I think I may even have elbowed Mark during my celebrations.

The second half flew past but it was also nerve wracking and both sides had chances to turn the tide or finish the match off. A blow of the final whistle and we're all on cloud nine, MyFC and the Ebbsfleet originals celebrating together. Then, celebrations over, we make our way back to the party. I was stopped outside by a female; if you're reading this then I'm sorry but I've no idea who you were. At the party it was a case of meeting more people and, finally, getting a chance to spend some time with Will Brooks. We chatted about MyFC, pre-season in Scotland and My Football Club in Scotland but most importantly it was good to get that real connection. There was also the North vs South football match, the North won 2-1 with my good self setting up the winner and Ockers scoring a goal which wouldn't have looked out of place a mile over the road. Least said about my hotel room the better.

May 11 2008

Well, who'd have thought it? It was good to see Noah and CamK again, Ozjohn didn't make it for some reason and, sadly, Sarah-Jane couldn't get down. I can't wait for the new season to start, a wee tour of Scotland would be a great start and we've got Wrexham and Barrow to look forward to. It'll be by bus though, I've had enough of sitting in airport departure lounges as my flight is postponed again and again. Not sure we'll let Grantwilson07 on though, apparently a UEFA Final is more important than the FA Trophy. I'll say goodnight and thank you here, hopefully my ears will pop before I wake up tomorrow. ☺

KENNY MORRISON (ManicScot)

○ **The flags flutter after the final whistle** NATHAN HENDLER

CHAPTER 11

A FAMILY
DAY OUT

◠ **Well deserved winners!** MATTHEW PEARCE
◑ **Torquay fans gone, Liam takes trophy on jumbo-tron** NATHAN HENDLER
◑ **A magic moment for Slatts and Macca** TOM BROOKS

◑ **Eoin's first Mexican Wave**
EUGENE KING-HAUGHEY

The beginning. "Husband, what are you doing?" "I'm buying a share in a football club." "You're what? Have you gone completely mad? Who are you buying?" "I don't know. But there'll be thousands of us clubbing together to buy a club and run it." "Sounds like a great scam... Always knew a fool and his money were easily parted. Well, you carry on, Husband, and don't forget I want tickets for me and the kids when you get to Wembley."

Wifey walks away shaking her head, smiling to herself at the ludicrous idea. I thought we might be there sooner than your beloved Geordies, Pet Lamb.

The trip down to Wembley. I woke up at 3:30am and had a strange feeling in my stomach. Not the usual urge for the loo, but butterflies. I was actually nervous about the game. Worried about a team I had never seen in the flesh and was less than twelve hours away from the biggest game in their history.

I turned over and tried to get some more sleep but it proved fruitless. I got up at 5:30am. Wifey was not stirring. I went in to check that the kids were sound asleep and then went downstairs and printed off some posters for the back windows of the car.

'Follow us and The FLEET to Wembley!!'
'Give us a toot for EBBSFLEET!!'
'We want to be in that number, when the FLEET go sailing in.'

I woke everyone up at 6:45am and the excitement started to grow. The children – Niamh 7, Seamus 5 and Eoin 3 – knew that it was a big day but were not sure what to expect.

"Dad, who are we playing today?", asked Seamus. "Torquay, son." The little one started to giggle. "We can't play Turkeys!!!" We all smiled and ⟫

Liam comes down the steps with the giant trophy
RUSSELL CUPITT

our opponents got their unflattering nickname for the day. Wifey got the kids ready while I packed that car and by 8am we were set for the long journey from sunny Runcorn to Wembley. "Are we really going to be away all day?", asked Niamh. "I hate football." Not a good start to the day I thought.

The first part of the journey went very quickly as we taught the children some songs to sing:

Tell me Mam, and Dad
I won't be home for tea
I'm going to Wemberlee
Tell me Mam, and Dad

Wemberlee, Wemberlee
We're the great Ebbsfleet United
And we're off Wemberlee
Wemberlee, Wemberlee...

Oh when the Fleet
Oh when the Fleet
Oh when the Fleet come sailing in
I want to be in that number
When the Fleet come sailing in

Just past Knutsford Service Station we get our first toot. We all looked up to see a car whiz past us, with the passenger kissing the badge on his shirt. Cheers all around. Thank God, we're not the only ones making this trip.

Wifey noticed that Radio Five Live had failed to mention the Fleet during their round-up of the day's matches, and promptly sent a text to them, informing them of the huge army of fans who were heading to Wembley from all over the world. They duly read it out and several more horn blasts follow. At this point, I was just beginning to get the feeling that it is going to be a great day.

Once inside the M25 we had our first meeting with the "enemy". I spied two minibuses decked out in yellow and informed the kids that they were full of "Turkeys". A chorus of boos rang out from the back seat as I drew up alongside them on the A40. Smiles emanated from everyone's faces at the cheeky rascals in the back. In order to focus minds again a 10p prize was offered to the first one to see Wembley's arch. Eager eyes scanned the horizon for it, and an argument ensued when everyone saw it at the same time... including Wifey! Cost me a fortune to avoid a riot. The remainder of the journey was straightforward and we found a convenient car park five minutes from the ground. Another chorus of boos rang out as we parked up. The poor parking attendants looked bemused in their yellow hi-viz jackets. The kids were unloaded and then dressed in the new Reds shirts. The boys had to have their faces painted red and white. They ended up looking like extras from Braveheart. Two young policemen were keen to have their faces done as well until a grumpy sergeant sent them on their way. By now Niamh had gone off to the other side of the car park with her new pompoms to choreograph her cheerleader routine for "The Fleet".

»»

○ Wifey and kids enjoying
the big day while Sacha
acknowledges the fans
EUGENE KING-HAUGHEY

The short walk to the stadium was a joy. Cheery waves to the coaches of Fleet supporters and manic boos at the Turkeys. As we approached Wembley, everyone was impressed at its size. All around the ground large groups of opposing fans stood chatting to each other, and on more than one occasion we were present when "virtual friends" from the MyFootballClub.co.uk forum met for the first time. We entered the stadium shortly before 1.30pm and made our way to Section 133. We walked slowly through the entrance and were overawed by the scale of everything inside. "This place is fantastic", said Seamus. "Beats St James' Park", I said to Wifey. Reluctantly she agreed but only after administering a sharp poke in the ribs for my cheek.

We sat down in our seats and were delighted at how good the location was. About 15 rows back, right behind the goal, and just above the height of the crossbar. The children were looking all around them, trying not to miss a thing, pointing out everything to each other. Then Ebbsfleet ventured out onto the pitch for their warm-up. The first time we had seen them in real life. The roar went up for the Reds. Eoin was apprehensive and hugged me tight, having never heard such a noise before. He soon relaxed and was shouting "Come on you Reds" at the top of his little voice. A camera crew and Captain Hooky – the mascot – walked around in front of the Ebbsfleet fans. The children raced down the terraces to meet him and were delighted to be caught on camera for the

whole stadium to see. The perfect cue for Niamh's routine but unfortunately she was a little late to catch the crew's eye. By now the stadium was filling up and it was very evident that Ebbsfleet would have the greater support. Half of the lower section was red as were several blocks of seats "up in the gods".

Time moved quickly on and before we knew it the teams were coming out for the start of the game. A quick check of the team showed that 10 out of my 11 selections were in the starting line-up. Looks like that Liam Daish fella and I are thinking along the same lines, I thought.

The game kicked off and Torquay began by putting Ebbsfleet under immense pressure in the opening stages. A superb save from Lance Cronin early on, some fortunate misses and determined tackling by the defence throughout the first twenty minutes saw Ebbsfleet remain on level terms. Following one Ebbsfleet attack, I looked across at my family and saw that they were all engrossed in the game, even Niamh! By the half hour mark, confidence appeared to be building amongst The Fleet fans around us and the singing started in earnest. Surprisingly, the boys picked up the words very quickly and Wifey and I had to smile as we saw our 3 and 5 year olds pointing and shouting "Who are ya, who are ya???" at the Torquay fans.

With 40 minutes on the clock, Chris McPhee slipped a great ball through for Luke Moore. He reached the ball just before Martin Rice, the goalie, ➤➤

THE FA CARLSBERG TROPHY
WINNERS 2008

THE FA CARLSBERG TROPHY
WINNERS 2008

⊕ **Let the celebrations begin...** THOMAS SYNNOTT

and was brought down. The ref had no choice but to give a penalty. Holding both lads up so that they could see, we watched as one as McPhee raced up and struck a firm shot towards goal but it was brilliantly saved. Disappointment all round as we sat down but the action continued. Then, just before half time, Sasha Opinel sent a long ball into the corner. John Akinde wouldn't allow the defender to shepherd the ball out and won it. A nippy run into the box, a short sharp pass across the face of the goal and there was McPhee in the right place to slot it home.

Everyone erupted in celebration. Complete strangers hugging and dancing with each other. Seamus stood on his seat waving his flag like crazy. Niamh was a blur with her pompoms, and poor Eoin was squashed in the hug between Wifey and myself. Almost instantly, half time was blown and everyone had time to catch their breath.

In what seemed like no time at all, both teams were out and the action started again. Ebbsfleet kicking towards their fans. To and fro, real end to end stuff. It was a good, hard, tight game. Opportunities arose around each goal and the excitement grew amid the fans. In what I took to be a sign of confidence, the Ebbsfleet fans started a "Mexican Wave". It started on the right-hand side of the Ebbsfleet following and worked its way around the ground, building momentum through the Red hoards. Until it reached the "Turkey" fans where it stopped dead. They were not happy bunnies and were not going to play. Another one

was started, the cheer louder than the last. When Torquay's fans failed to respond this time, they were subjected to a shower of boos. The children loved this and amused everyone around when they tried to start their own wave. These waves were to keep them occupied for the remainder of the game – that and shouting at the "Turkeys" whenever they fouled one of our players. "Hey ref, that's a foul. He was tripped", shouted Seamus. It was great to see them getting so passionately involved.

As the minutes ticked away on the scoreboard, the tension grew unbearable. When 90 minutes appeared on the screen we all stood closer together, holding each other tightly and shouting for the ref to end the game. Three long minutes passed and then it happened. The ref blew his whistle and Ebbsfleet had won the FA Trophy.

All around, people were ecstatic. I was so happy for the true, long-standing fans that they had seen their team win a big trophy for the first time and also for the new legends of supporters who, like me, had joined this crazy, wonderful scheme last year.

As we watched the team go up to collect the trophy, I looked at my family as they stood beside me, clapping, flag waving, singing and jumping for joy. I called over to the haze of pink pompoms at the end of the row and asked Niamh if she has enjoyed it. "It's brilliant, Dad. Can we come here again?", she said. "I hope we can, love.", I replied. ✍

EUGENE KING-HAUGHEY – Im Sportacus

CHAPTER 12

MY DAY AT
WEMBLEY WITH
NOTEBOOK
AND PEN

The boys have got to Wembley for the first time in their history and players, staff and supporters check their maps for the best route to take them to the 'Home of Football'. But for a large swathe of the media who have to cover The Fleet in the FA Trophy Final it's a case of: Where is Ebbsfleet? One reporter said to me: I've *Googled* it, and it's not altogether obvious.

I know Torquay is in Devon as I've been on holiday in the English Riviera but where the hell is Ebbsfleet?

That frustration set the tone for the afternoon for those hacks that are more used to covering Didier Drogba's goals for Chelsea than Chris McPhee's penalties for The Fleet.

So for those of you who are not part of Her Majesty's Fourth Estate, here is 'My day at Wembley with notebook and pen' by Paul Lagan aged 49 and a few days...

Once I had become a fully-fledged signed up for two years member of MyFootballClub.co.uk, Ebbsfleet United FC became my second team and I religiously checked for their scores. The first, my beloved Chelsea, I'm fortunate enough to follow in my professional capacity so getting down to Stonebridge Road is a problem during the season. So, when Aldershot were firmly dispatched in the semi-final stage, I quickly went onto the Internet and checked out The FA's media accreditation website. As a bone fide hack, I am registered for FA matches and so I placed my request for a media

pass and waited for the email to return a few days later that confirmed a seat for me in the hallowed press box.

So the day arrived. I, like thousands of my fellow – some albeit new – Fleet fans took the Tube to Wembley Park and sauntered down Olympic Way and all that awaited inside. With 'The Gulls' and 'The Fleet' fans directed up the walkways to their respective sides of the ground, the media continue straight on, remaining on ground level. It's then a sharp right, follow the media signs and the door to the stadium beckons. After showing my press card to the good folk from the FA's media department and collecting the sought-after media pass which hangs around one's neck and picking »

up a free programme, £3 is good value I hope, I pass a security guard who, in true airport style, gets me to empty my pockets of metal and scans my body with a fancy wand detector. Having decided I was not a terrorist threat, oh! but the power of the pen, I went in a lift to take me to the second level of the ground and into the corridor to take me to the press section.

The stadium is just a year old and the smell of the cream paint on the walls is still there. The media area is divided into two sections, east and west, which divides the halfway line in the middle tier of the stadium and can accommodate several hundred media very comfortably. One section, east, was closed off for a corporate event so the assembled hacks and hackettes were placed in west section. Both sections are identical, if mirror images of each other. Each comprises a large seating area where dozens of journalists can file their copy pre-and post match in peace. Then there is the eating area: yeah, we get free food and drink as well! It's tough being a football hack. In my case, a hot vegetarian option took my eye. Add to that a bread roll and salad and an orange juice from the bar and I was ready for my pre-match ritual of tucking into scran whilst reading the match programme.

At 1.45pm it was time to find my seat and prepare for the game. Looking around the press box, there were a few familiar faces and lots of people I've never seen on the professional-level of football circuit before.

We were with the Fleet fans so all around me was a sea of red. Journalists who shall remain nameless for fear of embarrassment, bombarded me with questions about my team.

The aforementioned where is Ebbsfleet was a prime example. Having volunteered enough information to allow the reporter to fill a 600-word report in one of the following day's national newspapers, I concentrated on the match; the half-time sandwiches and then the full-time whistle and trophy-wielding celebrations.

As we know, Daish's Darlings, as I coined them, won the match thanks to Chris McPhee's ❯❯

THE FA CARLSBERG TROPHY

WINNERS 2008

45th minute piece of magic. The fact he missed a penalty minutes earlier and was a former Torquay player gave the media a hook for their reports and the dream of the cup going to Kent became an extraordinary reality.

Now, football reporters are normally a cynical bunch and it's not form to jump up and down even if it's your team that's won. But your heart has to go out to one particular hack in row B in front of me, who I presume was a local reporter for Ebbsfleet United, who, when the final whistle blew jumped from his seat, punched the air and proceeded for the next 15 minutes to non-stop clap his team off the pitch, up to collect the cup and back to the pitch for the on-field antics. Heavy breathing complemented the tears rolling down his eyes, as I'm sure he will, like all of us, remember The Fleet's first and victorious trip to Wembley. "Where's the press conference held, mate" was the final question I needed to answer which one lost-looking hack asked me that warm, sultry afternoon. I took the reporter with me through the door that, after showing our accreditation to a security guard, allowed us access to Wembley's warren of hidden corridors. Thankfully, after only going down a couple of flights of stairs we were ushered into the conference room that resembled a Victorian operating room but much better furnished.

I sat in the back row looking down at the operating table behind which the mangers would sit and have their answers dissected by the media.

Many of the quotes seen in the Sunday and Monday newspapers would come from here. Player quotes would come from what's called the Mixed Zone area. This is a corridor, one level further down that links the players' changing rooms to the car park that houses the team coaches. The players would, if they wanted, stop and be interviewed by reporters. The victorious would, of course, talk for England. The vanquished, on the other hand, suddenly find their mobile phones red hot and pretend to be talking to someone as they gesture that they can't stop and scurry off to the comfort and safety of the coach. I dare say that I don't blame them but we hacks do love a quote. An hour after the match and the crowd has melted away, cheering or commiserating with each other. But back at the stadium many hacks are still at it; filing copy to their news desk. Some have had to write and rewrite match reports for various editions of their papers. Others are taking quotes off others who went to the Mixed Zone while they write their match report. It can be several hours before their day is over. Drained by their professional exertions they then trot off home back down the now empty Olympic way to the Tube station.

But they can claim their words will be immortalised in print for generations to view in newspapers or on websites or, like this, in book form. They can justifiably say they were there the day The Fleet won The FA Carlsberg Trophy at Wembley. ⚽

PAUL LAGAN – ruudboy

CHAPTER 13

EVEN SOUTH EASTERN TRAINS JOINED IN!

↻↻ The Fleet came sailing in - but by Tube, not boat. Wembley Way full of Fleet fans sailing home - fantastic!
DAN SCHUETTE, ANDY BROWN
↻ Chris McPhee heading down the tunnel at the end of the game   IAN BYERS
↻ The Emptying of Wembley
KEITH HANDLEY

Saturday May 10 was the day when a club owned by 30,000 Internet users took on a traditionally run club that had just missed out on promotion. Torquay United v Ebbsfleet United was an emotional roller coaster of a day. Both sets of teams and supporters no doubt experienced many highs and lows. Torquay had lost their promotion battle and were hungry to avenge that. Ebbsfleet started as the underdogs; they fought hard, strong and proud.

This time the underdogs came through to win by one goal to nil.

The day started at 8.00am, discussing tactics, possible team sheets and general Ebbsfleet stuff, over a nice fry-up. Then over to the train station to hear chants like "oh, when the fleet..." "Liam Daish's' Barmy Army..." and many more! Amongst all the chants, and laughter, there was an undertone of belief that a small club compared to Torquay could pull off a win. On the way up to Wembley, the trains were covered (inside) in red and white. Even the train drivers seem to be getting into the sprit of things. When pulling into Charing Cross the driver came on the tannoy and wished the team good luck!

On the tube, there was a mixture of red, white and yellow and the fans laughed and joked in good sprits about the coming game. As we got closer to the ground itself the laughing and joking seemed to subside. Both sets of fans went to different pubs to enjoy a few drinks before the match. There was only one main subject of conversation; the pending match, possible scorelines and who the scorers would be. On the way to the ground, there was a tense nervousness that hung in a cloud over the fans. When in the ground, by the food courts and souvenir stands, as people began to walk out on to the terraces their first words were "Wow"; the venue and the view just took everyone's breath away.

After all the months of training, preparation to organise nearly 25,000 people from over the world »

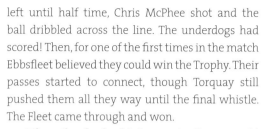

come to Wembley to support the underdogs and another 15,000 to support the favourites, the time was finally here to be hurled up, down, left and right on a roller coaster of emotions as both teams battled it out to win the match. Then, just before half time, a penalty! All through the stadium there was a tense silence as Chris McPhee placed the ball on the spot. The Fleet fans breathed a sigh of relief, knowing he had not missed a penalty all season! The ref blew the whistle; McPhee ran up, kicked and... saved! The Fleet fans started to believe that this wasn't going to be their day. With five minutes left until half time, Chris McPhee shot and the ball dribbled across the line. The underdogs had scored! Then, for one of the first times in the match Ebbsfleet believed they could win the Trophy. Their passes started to connect, though Torquay still pushed them all they way until the final whistle. The Fleet came through and won.

When the final whistle went, all you could hear where chants of "Liam Daish's' Barmy army..." and "Oh, when the fleet..." Just looking round the stadium you could see men, women and children in tears of jubilation. Walking out of the stadium you could see a whole array of emotions ranging from unquenchable joy, excitement and jubilation right through to the other end of the spectrum with those in yellow looking gutted, empty and disappointed.

Back at Northfleet train station all you could see was red and white – flags, t-shirts, banners and scarves. Walking through the town it was more like the carnival that you would expect if Ebbsfleet had won the FA Cup, not the FA Trophy!

As the days and weeks pass, Fleet fans still sit back and remember the game. Every now and then the slightest smile of joy at the thought "we did it" still appears on people's faces.

As the team looks forward to the new season, everyone who is involved in Ebbsfleet, is looking forward to the prospect of being promoted or even winning the FA Trophy again. The future is bright; the future is red and white. 🌀

TOM BYROM – trumpet

⌒ Ian Byers was fortunate enough to catch Sacha Opinel's left boot which he threw into the crowd as he was going down the tunnel at the end of the game   IAN BYERS

Celebrating at Baker Street tube – the happiest pic of the day
JEFF CHICK

Will meets the club's latest member…
RENE KUNISCH

CHAPTER 14
OUR DAY
IN THE SUN

Never in our wildest dreams could we have guessed that we would have been Wembley winners in May 2008 when back in the October 2007 we were playing guess the team almost every night. But due to some twist of fate, or maybe due to the hard work we put into this project to support the efforts of the long term fans, it was to be our day in the sun.

What a day it turned out to be. I know the word perfect is sometimes overused but I think we can use it in our case. Thanks to the efforts of Flash, a member from Inverness, we had a local sports club booked where we could all meet up, show each other our flags, talk, have a bit of a singsong and generally bask in the sun before heading towards the stadium.

Talking to my daughter, I agreed with her that the fact that families were there added to the day's events. They were in a safe environment, they could have a coke, play on the bouncy castle, run around and generally be a kid. New friendships were made between the young folk and that has to be a bonus for the future. To be a kid on your own at a do isn't much fun but get four kids together on a sunny day and the world is looking good.

Back in the big kids world, many of us 40-year-olds were getting ready to be 18 again. This is something that happens when you go to Ebbsfleet matches. There were members there from countries across the globe and they all had one thing in common, big smiles and the knowledge that we are involved in something special. If I had to award a smile of the day award then it would have to go to our friend from Turkey.

The game itself was a wonderful experience but others will tell you all about that. What many don't know is that there was a second big match at Wembley Park Sports Club. The MyFC North beat MyFC South and that may be commented on for months to come if Dixie gets his way.

This project keeps throwing up strange and wonderful things. As I sat there on the grass in the early evening sunshine, Trophy heading back to Kent and a nice tea in my belly, the world was looking a wonderful place. I was there talking to a guy from Sweden when the subject of members ⟫

↻ Fleet Glory Hunter, taken at the Big Meet
JEFF CHICK
↻ Picture from the Big Meet, taken after our great victory
NICK FISK
↻ Meg, Miss Yorkfox, the legendary red toothbrushes and Howezy getting in on the act
MARTIN THIRKETTLE
↻ Enginsan meets a fellow member at the pre-Wembley meet
KEITH HANDLEY

Smiles all round after the game...

JOHN HORVATH

The Big Meet before kick-off

NATHAN HENDLER

Niamh has pompoms, Seamus & Eoin all painted up

EUGENE KING-HAUGHEY

Bjhammer meets Will at the after game meet LORRAINE HANDLEY

Katie and Shooter DAN SCHUETTE

Manicscot is interviewed by Sparkyer for the MYFC Podcast KEITH A. HANDLEY

The big picture of the Big Meet GARY ROZANSKI

helping to move the project forward came up. As always, a simple statement ended up with a wonderful answer. I said that all members have talents and that we should use them in the nicest possible way. Another member laughed and said that he is a neurosurgeon! I got a bit nervous as he looks my way and, in my mind, I could see him drawing lines on my bald head to show him where to start!

It was great to have Will, Cal and Leyton with us during the evening. I felt for Will as even on the night of the Fleet's great triumph the press want a word on the phone, then us members all have to give him our opinions basically because he is there and we can. Leyton, you brush up pretty good dude!

The general atmosphere of the evening was so relaxed and full of fun. We proved that Mark is taller than Cana, and learned that cameraman Harry could take on Manic Scot at wrestling if you give him a few glasses start. The social side of MyFC is proving to be very positive and fun. I believe we should have a do on the last Saturday home game before Christmas and also on the last Saturday home game before the end of the season.

The highlight of the day for me happened over 100 miles north of Wembley. It was nearly midnight as Lorraine and I walked into a motorway service station proudly wearing our Fleet trophy final shirts. We passed two young lads and one said to us, 'Who won?' Lorraine replied, 'Ebbsfleet 1-0'. The guy then went, 'YES!' as he punched the ≫

⤸ A glorious evening at the Big Meet
DAN SCHUETTE
⤴ MarkRowly and Canagoon relax at the after match meet
KEITH HANDLEY

⤸ Corrie Jambo and FNEX   FLASHMEISTER
⤸ Callum and Charlotte at the meet   JANET RIMMER

air! What was that all about? Maybe two Kent lads away from home or is our support quietly getting deeper? Whatever the answer, it surprised us but in a wonderful way.

So, what comes next? The answer is hard work and to try and achieve a really wonderful thing. We have to build the club, the support and then have a real go at getting into the Football League. It was great fun going to Wembley but how much better it would be if we could go to Lincoln City, Gillingham and Accrington Stanley? We can do this and we have to aim for the highest possible standards in everything that we do. We have been to Wembley, seen the lads walk out onto the famous pitch and win against a team who had just had a very good season. When you consider what we did at Aldershot, should we be worried when we have to go to Stevenage, Mansfield Town or Wrexham? Call me overconfident if you like but I fear nobody after Wembley. Yes, we have to respect the opponents but I think we can give anybody a game now.

Finally, as I walked toward the ground pre-game, a few Torquay United fans were singing a really clever and unique song, one that we must have only heard and read a few hundred times. 'Cyber fans, you're only cyber fans!' For some reason, I said loudly as I walked on briskly, "30,000 cyber fans!"

If we work together, 10 may 2008 will only be the first of our glorious days in the sun. ☺

KEITH A HANDLEY – yorkfox

↷ Jude and Anna add a bit of glamour to the day   DAN SCHUETTE
↻ Bakert makes himself known
KEITH A. HANDLEY
↻ The Phantom Sheep & Flash
LORRAINE HANDLEY
↪ Shooter shoots... and scores
DAN SCHUETTE
↺ An emotional day under the Wembley Arch – and it all gets a bit much   ANNA BROOKS
↻ Grass, tyres, beer... And Fleet Fans, too !   DAN SCHUETTE

EPILOGUE
THE PRIDE
OF KENT

SPECIAL THANKS TO THE FOLLOWING SUBCRIBERS WHO HELPED TO MAKE THIS BOOK POSSIBLE: GLYN ABBOTT   DAVID ADAMS   JOHN ALDRIDGE   LEE ALLAN   CRAIG ALLEN   KEVIN AMIS   JORGE ANTUNES   WILLIAM ARTIGLIERE   DONY ASDONO   DAVID AZCUÉNAGA LASTRA   SIMON BAALHAM   SIMON BACHE   MARK BAGLEY   MARK BAILEY   NICK BAINES   OSWIN BAKER   BJØRN JACOB BAKKE   TIMOTHY BALL   MICHAEL BARBER   JON BARRATT   ANN BARRY   ROBERTO BAVA   NICK BEADLE   DESMOND BEARDS   DAVID BELCHER   ROBERT BENSON   CHRIS BERKELEY   JENS BESSERMANN NIELSEN   DEREK BEVAN   HEATHER BIAS   KARE BJORKLUND   LARS OLAV BJØRNSTAD GJØVIKLI   WILLIAM BLACKMAN   HELMUT BLUM   PAUL BOAK   STEVE BOEM   MARTIN BOGUE   JELMER BOOTS   HEIKO BOTT   GRAHAM BOWDERY   RICHARD BOWER   DEREK BOWRA   MICHAEL BOWRA   SUSAN BOWRA   ROBERT BOYCE   CHRISTEL BRACKE   PAUL BRESLIN   ANDREW BRETT   THE BRICK   MATTHEW BROMLEY   PAUL BROOKER   WILL BROOKS   JULIE BROOM   ANDREW BROWN   CRAIG BRYAN   ROBERT BUDGE   GARRY BUNDOCK   PAUL BURNETT   JOHN L BURNLEY   IAN BURRIDGE   TINA BUTTON   IAN BYERS   THOMAS BYNG   WENDY CAMPBELL   ALEX CARLOSS   PHILLIP CARTER   DEREK CAUDWELL   MARCO CELON   MARTIN CHARD   IAN CHARLTON   JAMES A K CHARLTON   PAUL CHARNOCK   TERENCE CHECKLEY   GARY CHEESEMAN   ROBERT CHESTER   JEFF CHICK   ANDREW CHYBA   DIEGO CIANFLONE   SJ CLARIDGE   ANDY CLAYTON   NIK CLEMENT   ANDREW COCHRAN   IAN COCKERILL   ANNA COLLIE   STEPHEN COLLINSON   SHARON COMMINS   ANDREW COOKE   RICHARD COOKE   DANNY COOPER   LAURIE COOPER   MIKE COOPER   EDWARD COPPEN   MICHELE CRAWFORD   WILLIAM CRICHTON-STUART   DAVID CROSBY   BARRY CROWN   JOSELITO CRUZ   RUSSELL CUPITT   KENNETH DALHAUG   PEDRO DANIEL DAMASO RAPOSO   ANTHONY DAVENPORT   DAVID DAVIS   GUY DAVIS   PAUL DAY   ADRIAN DELLICOTT   BRUNO DELORME   RAY DERKACZ   JAMES GRAY DEWAR   ANDREW DIGNAM   DISCREETWARE   HÅKAN DOHSE   SPENCER DOLMAN   NEIL DOUGLAS   JOHN DRISCOLL   PETER DUFFELL   STEVE EAST   DAVE EDMONDS   PAUL EDWARDS   RICHARD ELDRIDGE   ALAN ELFORD   ØIVIND MAGNUS ENSBY   PAUL ENSELL   ALBERTO ESPAÑA GONZALEZ   ROEL ESSELINK   JOHN EVES   AKMAL FARIMAN   ROY FARTHING   ADRIAN FELSTEAD   MAURICIO FERREIRA SANTANA   CHRIS FIELD   ANDREW FINLAY   NICK FISK   BRIAN FITZGERALD   LARS FLATEBY   DANIEL FLIES   DUNCAN FLOUNDERS   KEITH FOX-HAMMOND   JANENE FRANCIS   CHRISTINE FRANKLIN   MARK FRASER   JAMES FREED   JOSHUA FRIEDMAN   GLENN FULLER   INGRID FULLER   KATHRYN GALE   MARK GAMBLE   SIMON GAMBLE   AARON GANZ   ANDREW GARWOOD   JIM GEATCHES   CRAIG GIBBARD   TONY GILLEY   GIANFRANCO GIORDANO   BRIAN GLOVER   KEVIN GLOVER   DEAN GODDARD-HARDING   RICHARD GOLDBY   PAUL GOLDSMITH   AMANDA GORNALL   ROSEMARY GORVAN   TIM GREEN   WILLIE GROSHELL   GARY GROUTAGE   DAVID GRUNDY   GUILHERME GUIMARAES   BJÖRN GUSKE   RUDIGER GUSSETT   RIKU HAKULI   JONATHAN HALL   JULIAN HALL   CLIVE HAMILTON   JUERGEN HAMMER   KEITH A HANDLEY   LORRAINE HANDLEY   ANDREW HARDY   PHILIP HARRIS   MARK HARRISON   NICK HARRISON   MARTIN HART   RICHARD HART   DAVID HARVEY   MARY HAYDEN   PETE HAYLES   STEVE HEALY   GARETH J HEDLEY   CULLEN HENSHAW   ROXANNE HENSHAW   STEPHANIE HENSHAW   TALLULAH HENSHAW   MICHAEL HEUSER   ROB HEWISON   TOMMI HIETANEN   JACK HOLLIS   LEE HORROCKS   KEVIN HORTON   DAVID HOSKINS   GLEN HOSTETLER   JACK HOWES   CHARLES HUNT   SIMON HURLEY   LARS HYLAND   ERIK INGEBRIGTSEN   SEAN INGRAM   LYNDA IRVING   CHRISTOPHER JACKSON   CORRIE JAMBO   STEPHEN A JAMES   JAKE DAVID ALEX JARVIS   NEIL JEFFERY   TREVOR JOHN   ANDREW JOHNSON   ANDY JONES   PHIL JUDGE   JAMES R KAIGHIN   CHRIS KALMAR   RANDY KATZ   JOHN F KAY   MICK KEATING   JUSSI KEINONEN   VINCENT KELLY

BRETT KENNESON   STEVE KESTERTON   EUGENE KING-HAUGHEY   GEIR KJELLEVOLD   MICHAELA KLINGBERG   JOHN VON KLOPP   GARY KNIGHT   HANS JÖRGEN KNUTSEN   CHRISTOPHER KRAUS   DOUGLAS KUHN   STEVE KUNZER   KENNETH KUTA   PETER LANGTON   STUART LATHAM   SAMUEL LATULIPPE   NIGEL LAVERICK   GRAHAM LAVIS   CHRIS LAWRENCE   DAVID LEAHEY   ALAN STEPHEN LEAN   DAVID LEES   SCOTT LEIGH   DAVID LEWIS   DAVID STEPHEN LIGHTBOUND   PHILIP LIMB   MARK LINDOP   ANDREW LOWERY   DONAL LYNCH   SALVATORE MACCULI   JAY MALLORY   KATHRYN MANN   COLIN MANWARING   MICHAEL MARSH   MICHAEL MARSHALL   MARTIN MARTENSSON   ANGELA MASSIE   RAYMOND MAYS   MICHAEL MCDOWALL   JOHN MCKAY   ALEX MCMORLAND   JOHN MELDORF   PEDRO MELLO E CRUZ   MERILYN MELROSE   MGK TRADING CORP.   ALAN MILES   ED MILLER   H R MILTON   IAIN MITCHELL   MICHAEL MOATE   CHRISTINE MOLLOY   NICHOLAS MONKS   MATTHEW MORRISON   PHILIP MOSS   MIKE MOYES   GRAHAM MUIR   SIMON MULLISH   C F MUNNS   EMILIO MURCIA   GAVIN MURRAY   ANTHONY MUTIMER   PAUL NASH   CLARE NEILSON   NETMASTERY PTY LIMITED   STEPHEN JOHN NEWMAN   MICK NEWTON   SIMON NICOL   MATTHIAS NICOLAI   MICHAEL GORM NIELSEN   PER RICHARD NILSEN   SAM NISHI   NEIL OATLEY   F J O'CONNELL   JASON O'CONNELL   BARRY O'DONOVAN   PAUL O'FLAHERTY   BENJAMIN OGDEN   JOHN OKRAK   TONY OLIVER   ERIC OUTTIER   DAVID OWEN   N J PAINE   ALAN PALMER   JOHN PARKER   PAUL PARKINSON   JAN GLEN PAULSEN   CHRISTOPHER PAYNE   LES PEARSON   RICHARD PEARSON   STEPHEN PEGUM   CAITLIN PERRY   CLAIRE PERRY   FORDJ PICK   GRAHAM PILCHER   EVANS PIZAN   IAN PLEACE   STEPHEN POLLARD   CHRISTOPHER POVEY   MATT POVEY   MICHAEL JOHN POVEY   DAVID PRATT   DAVID PRESTON   TORSTEN PROFFT   ALAN PURCHASE   DAVID QUIBELL   MICHAEL QUILTER   JULIAN RABJOHN   BRAD RACETTE   JACQUELINE RANDOLPH   PETER RAWDING   IAN REARDON   CHRISTOPHER REED   GARY RICHARDSON   SHIRLEY RICHARDSON   TRACY RICHARDSON   STEVE J RIDGWAY   THE RIMMER   SANDRA RING   CLIFFORD ROBINSON   MICHIGAN ROCKETS   CHRISTOPHE RODRIGUES   JOHN ROGERS   MD ROWLINSON   DAVID E RUSCOE   CHARLES RUST   TIMM RUTLAND   DAVID W R RUTNAM   DENNIS RYAN   TONY RYDER   TONY SANDFORD   DOMENICO SANNA   PAUL SANTER   NICHOLAS SAVILL   ALAN SCAIFE   MARK SCHWARTZ   DOUGLAS R SEAL   STEPHEN SEATH   ROBERT SHEARD   DAVID SHEPHERD   J SHIMMIN   MARTIN SHURMER   GRAHAM SIDWELL   JONATHAN SILVESTER   IAN SIMPSON   BALBIR SINGH   SLA LTD   JAMES SMITH   JASON SMITH   JEFF SMITH   PHILIP SMITH   S J SMITH   SHARON SMITH   RUNE SOLEVÅG   KEVIN SOWTER   JAMES SPEED   LINDA STAFF   PETER STEVENS   LESLIE STEWART   MARTIN STEWART   DONNA STOCK   JAMES WILLIAM STONARD   MARC STORCK   LARS ERIK STORSTAD   GERALD STOUGHTON   JOSEF STROBL   PAUL SUMNER   KIRSTY TAYLOR   TRACEY TEMPLE   RUTH TERNENT   TOR TESSEM   MARTIN THIRKETTLE   JACQUELINE THOMPSON   BRONWYN THORN   ALAN TINGLE   JOHN TOULSON   MARK TOULSON   JARLE TRAAVIK   MICHAEL TRAINOR   PETER TRAVERS   RAJINDER S UPPAL   KAI VAADE   GARY VAUGHAN   JOHN VERLANDER   SHEHARA VISWANATHAN   THORSTEN DE VRIES   GARY WAGHORN   ABDUL HAFIZ WAHAB   SUSAN WAITE   JOHN WALKER   PHILIP WALKER   ROBERT WALKER   PER WALLEN   ALEX WALMSLEY   LEE WATERS   JON WEAR   CAROLINE WEBSTER   CHARLES WEBSTER   IAN WEEDON   KEVIN WEEKS   MARK WEISBERG   DAVE WENHAM   ALFIE WESTHEAD   BILLY WESTHEAD   DAVID WESTHEAD   IAN WHITTAKER   WARREN WILKINSON   JILL WILLERTON   C H WILLIAMS   BRADLEY WILMOT   STEPHEN WINDSOR   IAN WONNACOTT   ALAN WOODS   DERECK WOODS   JUSTIN WOODWARD   JANE WRIGHT   JIM WRIGHT   MELVIN WRIGHT   RON YAWORSKI   ANTHONY YEARWOOD   PHILIP YEATES   PATRICK YORK   DANIEL YOUNG   THOMAS ZAISS   MARCO ZARELLI   LOTHAR ZOK   **UP THE FLEET!**

⊃ Sacha Opinel on the Tube home after the game – sums up how hard the boys worked to reach the Trophy final, never mind win it!
SIMON BAALHAM

ACKNOWLEDGEMENTS

The publishers would like to thank the following for their invaluable contributions and support:

WORDS
Simon Denton (for his sterling work); the following for their glorious words: Tom Byrom; Paul Charnock; James Coulbault; Anthony Davenport; Josh Friedman; Willie Groshell; Keith A Handley; Eugene King-Haughey; Paul Lagan; Niall McNeill; Kenny Morrison; Dom Sanna; Graham Sidwell; Jim & Jane Wright

PICTURES
Special thanks to the following who contributed their beautiful images: Dave Plumb (EUFC); Matthew Ashton & Catherine Ivill (AMA Sports Photo Agency); Luis Javier Alvarez; Paul Apps; Simon Baalham; Mark Bailey; Jelmer Boots; Robert Boyce; Anna Brooks; Tom Brooks; Andy Brown; Tina Button; Ian Byers; Jeff Chick; Simon J Claridge; Anthony Coleby; Danny Cooper; David Crosby; Russell Cupitt; Kenneth Dalhaug; Anthony Davenport; Spencer Dolman; Terry Doran; Neil Douglas; Alan Elford; Steve Fair; Nick Fisk; Glenn Fuller; Kevin Glover; Tim Glynne-Jones; Graham Gordon; Jürgen Hammer; Keith A Handley; Lorraine Handley; Gareth Hedley; Nathanial Hendler; Cullen Henshaw; Mark Hodgkinson; John Horvath; Jack Howes; Eugene King-Haughey; Rene Kunisch; Simon Lowther; Chris Maw; Damian Mcgeady; Ed Miller; Max Newton; Matthew Pearce; Janet Rimmer; David Robson; Gary Rozanski; A W Scaife; Dan Schuette; Martin Shurmer; Thomas Synnott; Peter Taylor; Martin Thirkettle; Jarle V Traavik; Robert Walker; David Westhead

LAST BUT NOT LEAST...
Thanks to the MyFC web team (Callum, Duncan, Gary, Harry, Julia, Tim, Tom and Will) for your web pages, email blasts, pictures and backing.
Finally to the staff and players of Ebbsfleet United FC who made all our dreams come true on 10 May 2008. Cheers!